Because of a Promise

A Mother's Inspirational Journey from Whispers to Ripples

Sandy Cappelli

Because of a Promise

A Mother's Inspirational Journey from Whispers to Ripples

Published by
Sandy Cappelli
Upland, California
www.BecauseOfAPromise.com

Cover Design by Dan Mulhern Design
Interior Design by Dawn Teagarden
Interior flower designs by Alexa Cappelli

Unless noted otherwise, all Scripture quotations are taken from the New International Version (NIV) of the Holy Bible.

ISBN: 978-0-9884082-0-3 (paperback)

Printed in the United States of America
www.BecauseOfAPromise.com

To my awesome God…
You have blessed me in so many ways.

"For I know the plans I have for you," declares the Lord,
"plans to prosper you and not to harm you, plans to give you
hope and a future." Jeremiah 29:11 NIV

To my husband, Tony…
Thank you for believing in me…for believing in us.
I love you.

To my beautiful children, Nick, Alexa, and Steven…
You all bring me such joy and are my inspiration
for living a very different life.
I am so proud to be your mother.

Table of Contents

Introduction

No One Could Have Prepared Us

"Can you watch the kids for awhile?" I yelled over my shoulder as I hurried up the stairs.

I could hear squeals of delight from Nicolas and Alexa, and knew they were up to no good. They were in their highchairs, and Tony was reading the paper at the kitchen table. "Nicolas, don't do that with your bananas." Tony sounded more tired than amused. "Last time, they got stuck."

I had a plan for my life.

Nicolas loves entertaining his sister and, from the sound of Alexa's laughter, he was succeeding again. I didn't turn back to see what he was up to, but I chuckled thinking about the fate of the banana.

"Sandy, don't be too long," Tony called out in my direction. I didn't answer as I closed the door behind me. With the door shut, the voices downstairs were barely audible. This rare silence is something I usually cherish, but today I wasn't looking for peace and quiet.

There was something important on my mind, and I couldn't get my laptop open fast enough to begin typing these words:

"I heard a powerful church message this morning and I'm convinced God wants my story told. Although this spiritual ride began two years ago with the birth of our twins, the latest chapter of the tumultuous journey began a week ago when Tony and I went for a routine ultrasound to check the progress of my second pregnancy. What the doctors told us changed our lives forever..."

It's interesting how experiences can change the course of our lives. Like so many people, I had a plan for my life. I would go to school, start my career, get married, and start a family. My husband would have his career, I would have mine, and we would be involved in our children's activities. It would be a simple, but good life.

I was running my insurance agency, and my husband Tony was in the housing industry, neither of us focused on what the future might hold. I thought little about illness and even less about death. It was August, and my twin babies, Nicolas and Alexa, had just celebrated their first birthday. I was five months pregnant with my third child and scheduled for a routine ultrasound. No one could have prepared us for the diagnosis they were going to give our unborn child.

"Your son has a heart defect."

"Your son has a heart defect." The words spoken that fateful day still echo in my mind, even as I write this. And after a few weeks of testing, we would learn the devastating news that his condition was fatal.

It was at this same time that God began communicating a powerful promise involving my son's condition. As we struggled with the idea of delivering a child destined to die, God seemed to be asking us to trust in His plan. With no clear understanding of the path we were headed down, we made the challenging decision to complete the pregnancy and trust God with the outcome.

And so the journey began.

> We made the challenging decision to complete the pregnancy and trust God with the outcome.

What is written on these pages is not the story I intended to write. Whenever I altered the direction of my story to fulfill my own desires, God seemed to redirect my words. In my quest for understanding God's promise for my son, I was forced to face something bigger than life. And through this powerful yet humbling experience, a transformation of my own beliefs occurred. I learned that specific moments and experiences are given to us for spiritual growth and to challenge us to refine or redirect our life's path. What we do with these experiences can dramatically influence our destiny.

When I read the words I have written, I can hardly believe they are mine. In fact, I hardly believe it is my life. Until a few years ago, my religious beliefs were conservative and my relationship with God distant. I believed in Him, but had not been personally touched by His power. I was unfamiliar with the many ways God communicates. This incredible journey through skeptical eyes allowed me to experience an intimate God with whom I was unfamiliar.

Sharing the private details of my journey is difficult. *It is so personal.* It has taken me over ten years to embrace my new life and let go of the fears that have kept me from moving forward. In part, I've been reluctant to share my story out of concern of being judged on what could be considered a controversial topic — whispers from God.

But then, I had the opportunity to join a group study at our church called "The Power of a Whisper: Hearing God & Having the Guts to Respond," by Bill Hybels, a respected world-renowned pastor and transformational speaker. My heart was racing when I first heard that the title of his book was *The Power of a Whisper.* As I looked around the crowded room, knowing there were people all over the country and possibly the world doing this same study, I realized that a whisper-filled life is not as crazy as it sounds.

I immediately picked up the book and started reading the first few pages, where he wrote: "I have chosen to wait 35 years before writing a book about how God's whispers have affected my life — hesitant in part because of the controversy this subject tends to arouse." He expressed concern that people might think he had "lost his marbles," a feeling I also related to. And then he said, "So why go to the trouble of writing this book? Because I firmly believe that God whispers to you, too. If you lower the ambient noise of your life and listen expectantly for those whispers of God, your ears will hear them. And when you follow their lead, your world will be rocked." I closed the book and shut my eyes as if it was God Himself speaking those words to me…and I said, "YES."

That night, I went home and cried, knowing my life was about to change dramatically, as I was being called to take my next leap of faith in this life that God has planned for me. So I published this book and have begun to share my journey — that started with a whisper and ended with bigger ripples than I could have imagined.

We may never know the full impact of this story, but my prayer is that God speaks to others and guides them into deeper understanding of His promises as they witness my journey...

Sandy

Chapter 1

The First Promise

"A journey of a thousand miles begins with a single step."

~ Lao Tzu ~

Two Years Earlier

It was a persistent, sort of nagging feeling that wouldn't go away – nothing specific, just something I *knew* without knowing why. Although I didn't understand the specifics of this premonition, I believed it involved my ability to have a child. As far back as my early twenties, I was not even trying to conceive, and yet "it" weighed heavily on my mind for years.

Over a decade later, the painful reality of my premonition would come true. After spending two years trying various fertility treatments, my OB/ Gynecologist referred us to a reproductive endocrinologist for further testing. Sitting in front of a fertility doctor, going over the results of some tests, I realized nothing could have prepared us for his diagnosis.

"Your follicle stimulating hormones, or FSH levels, are elevated to an unusual level," he said, pausing before continuing. His voice was monotone, and he showed little emotion as he delivered the news. I found myself disliking him before he even finished his sentence. "FSH levels are used to determine proximity to menopause. As they begin to elevate, a woman's ovaries become less productive as they approach menopause."

He was silent, as if the silence might help us absorb the magnitude of what he was saying. *What does that mean? My ovaries aren't productive? I'm in menopause?* A million questions were swarming through my head, but no words were coming from my lips.

"It is a gradual process, during which it becomes more difficult to get pregnant as the ovaries produce fewer eggs and the quality of the eggs deteriorate. Eventually, the ovaries stop producing altogether. Based on your FSH levels, you have less than one-half of a one percent chance of becoming pregnant."

He paused again and scratched at his mustache. He was a thin man with sandy brown hair, whose wrinkled shirt and crooked tie made him look disheveled and unorganized. It did little for the way I felt about him.

We sat stunned in silence while he continued with the diagnosis. Even with the tears streaming down my face, there was no compassion in his voice or eyes. I wondered how many times he had delivered this kind of devastating news to couples struggling with infertility.

"Because the elevated FSH level is happening to you at age 35 instead of in your 40s when most women experience it, the condition is called Premature Ovarian Failure. It affects less than one percent of all women and can be linked to serious health problems, but often times, it is simply hereditary."

> We sat stunned in silence while he continued with the diagnosis.

I found myself drifting off and focusing more on the clutter on his desk and the depressing room we were in than on what was being said. The office wasn't clinical like you would expect. It was poorly lit with no windows, and there was nothing bright or cheerful in it. I'm not sure how long I stared at the framed picture of a tree that was hanging slightly off-center on the wall behind him.

In a daze, I heard neither the questions from Tony nor the answers from the doctor. Tuning back in just before he finished, I heard him say, "We should recheck your FSH levels for an error since the odds are so low that this would be happening to you." But based on the insight that had been with me for so many years, I had a sickening feeling it was accurate.

As we stood to leave, my eyes met Tony's for the first time since we had walked into the doctor's office. He was fighting back tears and glanced away quickly to keep his emotions under control. He shook the doctor's hand, and we walked out.

Neither of us spoke as we walked the short distance to the car. I buckled my seat belt and through tears murmured, "This feels like a really bad dream."

Tony reached for my hand and gave it a gentle squeeze before he quietly answered, "Let's not make any decisions until we confirm the results." I saw a tear roll down his face as we pulled out of the driveway.

Two weeks later, a second test confirmed the original results. I was at my office when I got the bad news, and although sad, I wasn't surprised. I had mentally prepared myself for the news and had convinced myself there would be other options to help us conceive. I began reading every book on fertility I could find, although it didn't take long to discover there are only a few choices for women facing this diagnosis:

1. an In Vitro Fertilization (IVF) method using my eggs and Tony's sperm,

2. an IVF method with donor eggs *(With this option, I would have embryos that were created from Tony's sperm and a donor's eggs implanted in me. I would be the biological mother giving birth to the child, but would have no genetic influence on the child unless the donor eggs were from a relative)*, or

3. adoption

When I pursued answers from a second fertility doctor, we were told that IVF has a very low success ratio (usually under 5%) with people who have elevated FSH levels as high as mine. This left us with the choice of IVF with donor eggs or adoption.

After hearing the fertility diagnosis and reviewing our options, I cried on and off for days. I was devastated that IVF with my eggs was not a viable option. *It feels like a part of me died with the diagnosis.*

We got a third opinion from another reproductive endocrinologist that only served to spiral me deeper into depression. Rage and depression flooded over me like a huge, drowning wave. I could not focus at work and stayed away from friends and family. I was unable to sleep at night, and then so tired in the morning and throughout the day that I was barely functional. I would cry out to God with questions that seemed to have no answers.

Who is to blame? God, why have You let this happen? Where are You in my time of need? Why have I known all these years that I would have trouble getting pregnant? Is this Your plan for me? And if it is, I hate it! Please, please don't let this happen to me.

Every baby I saw triggered an ache so deep that I felt physical pain. Stories I heard about children, particularly those involving neglect or abuse, deepened my sorrow and led to more unanswered questions. *Why are they parents and not me? This isn't fair.*

Picking Up the Pieces

Three weeks went by, and I knew I needed to pick up the pieces and move on. Every day or two, Tony would bring up the fertility topic, hoping to get me to discuss a plan, and every day, I would shut him down. He was frustrated, and I didn't care; I just wasn't ready to take the next step. I was grieving the loss of my fertility, like a parent might grieve the loss of a child, and was not receptive to any discussion.

But after three weeks, I knew I had to engage the conversation. *I have to pick up the pieces…for me and for us.*

"How was your day?" I asked as he came through the front door. He looked tired and depressed, even more than usual. It was late August, and the summer breeze blew through the house with the front door open. He set his briefcase down and picked up an envelope that had blown off the stack of mail he was balancing in the other hand.

"Okay, I guess." He closed the door, pulled his keys out of his pocket, and tossed them on the dining room table. "How are you doing today?" he asked as he was flipping through the mail.

"I'm ready to move on," I blurted out. Immediately, I had his attention, and he waited for me to finish my thought. After a long pause, I said, "I'm not getting help from God with any of my prayers, so I'm ready to make some decisions without Him."

Tony frowned at my sarcastic God remark as he walked over to sit down beside me on the couch. He set a piece of mail that he still had in his hand on the coffee table and turned my shoulders toward him so he could look directly into my eyes. "So what does that mean – that you're ready to 'move on'?"

We both knew we would be facing some turbulent times and difficult decisions in the near future.

"I'm willing to do adoption or IVF with donor eggs. Let's just do something." There was conviction in my voice for the first time in a long time. It felt good. "I'm a doer, and doing nothing is making me crazy. What are your thoughts on adoption?"

He was quick to respond, as though he had been waiting for the opportunity. "I'm open to the idea of adoption, but I want to try IVF first. If it doesn't work the first time, we will adopt." He continued to stare directly into my eyes, waiting for my reaction.

I could feel my eyes starting to tear, "But we won't have the money for adoption if we try IVF and don't end up pregnant."

"We will find it somewhere. Let's cross that bridge when we come to it." He put his arm around me, and I leaned into his embrace for comfort. We sat in silence for a few minutes. I think we both knew we would be facing some turbulent times and difficult decisions in the near future.

After a week of investigating fertility centers and doctors' IVF success ratios, I had made significant progress. We narrowed it down to three centers and finally decided on a fertility center in Los Angeles, a convenient forty-mile drive from our home in Upland, California.

Now to determine the donor.

To my amazement, my three sisters, my aunt, and a couple of close friends were all ready to donate eggs. We decided on my sister, Julie, mainly because she was the youngest, and the success ratio is highly dependent on the quality of the eggs, which is determined by age. The first step was to have her FSH levels tested to determine if she would make a good candidate. And, once again, I was asking for God's help.

Oh dear God, please help me with this huge decision. We don't know if using Julie's eggs is a really good idea or a really bad one.

Part of me liked the thought of using my sister's eggs because I would know the history and would have a baby who would be closely aligned genetically. But another part of me was very nervous and scared. *Are we too close? How will she feel when the baby comes? How will the child feel? We wouldn't keep this a secret from the child.*

Lord, please make this huge decision clear to us. We will listen.

It felt good to be talking to God again; it was too big of a decision to make without Him. I promised Tony I would be okay with whatever direction God pointed us in, although I was hoping deep down it would work with my sister's eggs.

Three days passed and my sister's FSH levels came back too high. It was another blow, but I believed it was also an answer to my prayer. I wasn't going to dwell on it. We immediately started looking at other options. I had heard of facilities that specialize in matching patients with egg donors, and was determined to stay focused on moving forward and finding the perfect donor.

I spent a few days on the computer and found a number of facilities that show women's profiles on the Internet. It became a project within a project for me, and I compiled a two-inch thick manual of information on egg donation.

An Unusual Phone Call

We had just come in from grocery shopping when I pushed the blinking light on the answering machine. "Sandy, my mom told me you are considering egg donation. I really need to talk to you before you make any decisions. Oh, by the way, this is Kim. Talk to you soon."

"Who was that?" Tony asked.

"My cousin Kim," I answered without elaborating.

I was trying to comprehend the message when Tony impatiently interrupted. "Kim?" He was looking for an explanation, confused at the idea that someone whose voice he did not recognize had some important information for us on egg donation.

"You know her," I assured him. "Kim is my cousin, currently living in Colorado, with her husband and four children. You met her at her brother's wedding when we were first dating. I'm pretty sure she was at our wedding, too."

Tony nodded as if he vaguely remembered while I continued to fill him in on the details. "We grew up together in California. As teens, our busy lives took us in different directions. Since she married and moved out of California, we haven't kept in touch. Weddings and funerals are the only times we see each other anymore," I paused and shrugged my shoulders, "and I guess there haven't been any weddings or funerals lately."

"Do you think she is offering to help us?" he asked, as he continued to put the groceries away.

I picked up the empty grocery bags he had tossed on the floor and threw them in the trash. Deep in thought, I didn't answer his question right away. It was hard for me to comprehend that a cousin who had become so distant over the years would even consider this. *But that's Kim, and that's why I love her. She is crazy - wonderfully crazy! And her faith in God is crazier still.* I walked over to the barstool near the sink and sat down, still trying to process the message she left.

"I don't think it's a good idea, even if she is offering," I finally replied. "It is an amazing gift, but I think we should stay away from using a family member. As much as I would love to have such a close genetic connection, I think there could be too many issues in the future." A couple of seconds later I added, "Besides, she is thirty-four, less than a year younger than me, so I think she is too old."

Tony agreed. Doctors stressed that we should find someone in their twenties for the greatest chance of success because IVF with donor eggs comes with a $15,000-$20,000 price tag. As it was, we would need to borrow money to cover the costs, so I wanted to do everything possible to increase our odds for success.

> This may be a lot for you to absorb, but this is all part of a much bigger plan. God's plan."

After a long silence, I stood up and walked back to the cordless phone. "I'm going to call Kim and politely decline, assuming that is what is on her mind." Tony didn't say anything as he grabbed the kitchen trash and walked out the French doors.

"Hi Kim…" I said, leaning against the kitchen sink.

I hardly got the words out of my mouth when she interrupted me. "Sandy, I know this sounds strange, but I have known for years that I would be donating eggs to help someone get pregnant. I thought it might be for my sister, but when my mom mentioned your situation, I knew it was for you."

I was stunned, and feeling a little faint, so I decided to get some water and sit down as I searched for my response. "I don't even know what to say to that. What do you mean you have known for a long time you would be helping someone get pregnant?" I finished filling my cup with water and sat down on the barstool.

"This may be a lot for you to absorb, but this is all part of a much bigger plan. God's plan." Her voice was steady and confident, but all I felt was confusion and stress. I stood up again and began pacing in the kitchen. I knocked my plastic tumbler full of water off the sink and didn't even bother to pick it up.

Tony came through the back door to see me walking in circles, clearly stressed out, with water all over the floor. He had a confused look and wanted to know what was going on, but picked up the tumbler and began wiping the water off the floor while he waited for me to finish the call. I let Kim talk for a couple more minutes before interrupting her, "I'll call you back, Kim. I need to talk to Tony."

As I filled Tony in on the details, I began pacing the kitchen floor again. He put his arm on my shoulder and led me out of the kitchen toward the stairs where we both sat down. "How in the world does she know this?" I was clueless as to what God's plan was for me, and had even more trouble comprehending her relationship with God. "How can she know she will be donating eggs? How does God communicate something like that?" I ranted with my hands gesturing toward the ceiling.

I started to stand up, but Tony stopped me. He took both of my hands into his and looked into my eyes. "Whatever you decide, I will support you," he said with sincerity, thinking he was being supportive. "This is a big deal, but I don't care if it's Kim's eggs or those of someone we don't know."

"What do you mean – you don't care whose eggs we use?" I snapped back, obviously missing his effort to support my decision. Tony realized he had said the wrong thing and tried to avert my glare.

"Honey, I just want you to be okay with the decision." He stood up to make a quick exit toward the garage.

With flailing arms, I chased him down the hallway. "But I'm not okay with this huge decision. This can't just be *my* decision! I don't want to be responsible for this decision." He ignored my ranting, and I chose not to follow him into the garage.

My thoughts swirled as I walked back to the living room. I couldn't think. *Does God want me to do this, or is Kim just being crazy Kim?* Her confidence stressed me out. *If I decide not to use her eggs and don't get pregnant, will I always wonder? How can I make this decision?*

I needed to call her back, but I didn't have an answer. I walked upstairs and sat on my bed, trying to decide what to tell her. About ten minutes of thinking brought me to the possibility of a compromise. I was still sitting on my bed when I called her back, blurting out my question without so much as a "Hello."

"How about getting your FSH levels tested before I stress out anymore about this decision? I'm not ready to say 'yes' or 'no,' but maybe God will make my decision clearer by then."

I was so frazzled that her cheerful response didn't improve my mood. "Sounds good to me. Seeing God's plan unfold is going to be awesome!"

Not knowing what else to do, I decided to pray. I was down on my knees in front of my bed begging. *God, as I have asked so many times, please make this decision clear to us.*

I was irrational but, as usual, Tony was practical. As he walked into the room and found me on my knees praying, he interrupted my desperate plea to God.

"So what's up?" he asked tentatively, having just come back from taking refuge in the garage. He seemed oblivious to the fact that I was in deep prayer.

Still on my knees, I quickly updated him. His response was, "Let's only accept very clear results, and any border-line results will be a 'no-go.'"

I nodded in agreement as I rose to my feet, "The doctor said the FSH needs to be 10 or less, so let's go with 9 or less."

A week later, Kim called with the news that her test results were a 7. I felt nervous excitement, but Tony was elated, with no reservations on moving forward. Even with my concerns, I had put the decision in God's hands, and believed a door had been opened for us to walk through.

And so our journey of faith continued.

A Big Setback

Everything was moving so quickly. It had been six weeks since Kim and I had completed preliminary testing and blood work. We were scheduled to start the medications and injections on November 5th, and the actual embryo implantation was scheduled for the first week of December. I was feeling positive about the upcoming procedure.

It was a warm Halloween day, and I was at my sister Lori's house with my younger sister Julie, my mom, and several friends. We were all sitting on the kitchen floor, carving pumpkins, when Lori's friend looked at Julie and asked, "So, how far along are you?"

Shocked, I glanced at my mother for confirmation, and her expression said it all. Julie was pregnant. My carving knife dropped to the floor as I jumped to my feet, ran through the living room to grab my purse, and headed out the door. My hand was covering my mouth. I wasn't sure if I was going to scream or throw up. My mom ran after me, asking me not to get in my car because I was too emotional. Not yet crying, I tried to convince her I was fine to drive as I climbed in the driver's seat and slammed the door. I knew I had to get away.

The car seemed to be on autopilot for several minutes until I decided to pull off the road. Although I wasn't crying, I realized I wasn't focused enough to be driving. Parked along the curb of a busy street, cars whizzed by, the drivers unaware of my

I was sick with anguish and mad at God.

moment of crisis. I sat in silence for about thirty seconds, and then there was no controlling the flood of emotion that followed. When the sobbing had ceased, the anger set in. My anger was not directed at Julie in any way. In fact, if I had been able to set aside my frustration with my own situation, I would have been happy for her. But in my emotional state of mind, I was sick with anguish and mad at God.

It made no sense to me. Julie wasn't even sure she was ready for another child at that time. Her desire to be pregnant was nowhere close to mine, yet she was pregnant, and I was not. *That's it. I'm not even sure I want to do this procedure!*

Still in my car, I yelled, *I am here God! Are You? Kim seems to believe You have a plan for me, but I sure don't get it. God, tell me WHY this is Your plan for me…if this really is Your plan for me. Is my flesh and blood not good enough for a child of God?*

My cell phone rang several times, but I didn't even look to see who was calling. I'm not sure how long I sobbed in my car, but by the time I got home, Tony was waiting for me. My mother had called him, and he had left his meeting early to get home. He ran outside to my car as I pulled in the driveway.

As my faith dwindled, I began looking more to statistics for answers than to God.

Seeing Tony's sympathetic expression triggered the tears again. The pain in his eyes was more than I could bear. "I don't know if I can do this," I cried.

"Do what?" He put his arms around me. I found comfort in his embrace, looking up into his dark brown eyes, but I couldn't keep the tears from rolling down my cheeks and smearing mascara all over my face and his shirt.

"I'm not convinced we should do the IVF," I said as I wiped my nose with the damp tissue I had pulled from my pocket. "I have lost so much faith that I'm not sure this is God's plan at all."

"Don't say that. Your sister's situation has nothing to do with us."

I snapped back, "What if we are not interpreting His signs accurately? What if they are not really signs from God at all? What if there is no baby?!?" I screamed.

He took my hand and walked me into the house. Knowing no words would console me, he sat on the couch with his arms around me and let me cry. When the tears finally subsided, I stood up and slowly headed toward the stairs.

"I'm going to bed," I murmured. My head was throbbing and my eyes were so red and puffy that I could hardly see my way up the stairs.

All night I struggled with whether or not to proceed. Surely, I would fall into a deep hole and never recover if no baby resulted from this journey of faith we were taking. *As it is, my odds are only 20 - 40% of getting pregnant, depending on the quality of the embryos,* I contemplated as I collapsed into bed. As my faith dwindled, I began looking more to statistics for answers than to God. *Adoption is looking better and better,* I thought as I lay in my bed with my eyes shut. And with that, I drifted into a deep sleep.

"We could take the $15,000-$20,000, use it for a private adoption, and be guaranteed a child," I said to Tony as he was getting ready for work the next morning.

Tony was trying to avoid a volatile reaction from me when he cautiously answered, "I think we should stay focused on everything we are doing. I believe God is with us on this."

As I began to protest, he picked up the phone and dialed someone on speed dial. His dark brown eyes were pleading with me as he handed the phone to me. "Please talk to Kim."

Kim had already said hello when I took the phone from him. She knew from caller ID that the call was from us. "Sandy…are you there?"

I immediately began ambushing her with my fears. "Kim, I'm not so sure anymore. What if this isn't God's plan?" Without giving her a chance to respond, I continued, "How can you be sure this is what God is communicating to you?" Tears welling up inside of me, my voice started to quiver.

She stopped me before I could spin completely out of control. "God has a plan for you and this baby He wants created. There is no doubt in my mind. Pray for answers, and you will hear Him. You will know like I know. You need to have faith in the Lord and this journey He is taking you on."

I was still not convinced and wanted to get off the phone. "I'll talk to you later Kim. I've got to get ready for work now."

I mulled over what she had said for the next couple of days and decided I had to continue with the IVF. It wasn't my belief that God was leading us that helped me to decide, as much as the thought that I never wanted to look back and wonder: What would have happened if I had trusted Kim's faith in God to continue this journey? Would there have been a baby? Did I disappoint God by not listening?

For most of my life, I have tried to live my life with no regrets on the "what if's" that come from not following one's heart. So although I made the decision to continue, I can honestly say that I felt no peace with it.

Have you ever had to put yourself in a place of trust, not knowing why, but knowing with all of your heart that it was the only thing to do?

Chapter 2

Two Miracles

"Before you were conceived,
I wanted you.
Before you were born, I loved you.
Before you were here for an hour,
I would die for you.
This is the miracle of life."

~ Maureen Hawkins ~

Something from God?

Kim and I started the injections as scheduled, but I continued to question God. *Where are you leading me? I'm worn out and so very tired.* I never thought to ask for peace, and I never felt it. The daily shots combined with the stress of worrying whether IVF was the right decision was wearing me down emotionally.

I was depressed and sleeping more than usual. There were days when I was overcome with sadness and only left my house to meet my mother who helped to administer my injections, twice a day, every day. It was difficult for her, but she never complained. Eventually, I was able to give myself the shots in my leg, but my mom still had to give me the ones in the hip. Neither mentally nor emotionally prepared for the long process of IVF, I was exhausted. I wandered into the insurance agency I owned daily, but my concentration wasn't there, so I didn't accomplish much.

Mid-November, Kim called with something on her mind. "Hey Sandy, how are you feeling?"

Not sure if she was asking about my mental or physical state, I decided not to mention the demons I battled every day while moving forward with our "plan." Instead, I tried to sound chipper. "I'm doing good, but sick to death of these shots already. How is it going on your end?"

"Great," she responded in her typical confident way.

I swear she takes "happy" pills before she calls me just to sound upbeat and keep me focused. She can't be having much fun either with all of this preparation for the egg retrieval and implantation.

"I have something for you," she said. "When I come out to California in a few weeks, I'll give it to you."

She sounded a little secretive, so I pursued it. "What is it?"

"Just a little something from God, but that's all I'm going to tell you for now. Oh, by the way, I had a dream. Two babies were lying in a crib. It looked like one was a boy and one was a girl." With more excitement in her voice, she nearly squealed the words, "I think you are having twins!"

Silence and doubt hung heavy on my end of the phone; I couldn't share her joy. I was too consumed with self-pity and the fear of not getting pregnant to even dream that two babies might be in my near future.

> I was afraid to have hope.

Kim continued to chatter, seemingly clueless of my doubts. "It wasn't clear, but I even sensed the presence of a third child." With laughter in her voice, she added, "Maybe triplets?"

"Bring them on," I said, lacking the conviction that one would expect with an upbeat response like that. I wanted to sound positive, but I just couldn't believe what she was saying. *Is it really possible for God to communicate with that kind of clarity?*

She waited for me to say more, but I was quiet. Finally, sensing my silence as doubt rather than pure excitement over her news, she quickly ended the conversation, "You'll see soon enough." When I didn't immediately reply, she said, "Gotta go! See you in a few weeks."

Once again, I found myself sitting on the stairs, unable to move and unable to comprehend the possibility of twins or triplets. *It seems ridiculous, but is it?* I was afraid to have hope.

For the next few weeks, I found myself thinking about what God had given her to give to me. More doubt. *How can she have something tangible from God?*

I anxiously awaited Kim's visit, and at the end of November, she came out to celebrate Thanksgiving and have the eggs extracted. When we got together the day before Thanksgiving for a visit, she was visibly uncomfortable while talking to Tony and me. We were at her parent's house, about an hour from our home, and we had just finished dinner. Uncle Jack was sitting next to her on the couch, while Tony and I were sitting in chairs across from them. Aunt Carol was still working in the kitchen.

"This may be hard for you to believe," she said as she reached into her jeans' pocket to pull something out.

I found myself getting nervous, just watching how uncomfortable she seemed to be. Anxiety also came from knowing this was going to top all of the other hard-to-believe things that Kim had told me. It was stressful knowing the sole basis for this journey was Kim's belief in God. I was making huge decisions based on *her* faith, which I had serious doubts about. I fidgeted with my wedding ring while waiting for her to retrieve whatever was in her pocket.

Finally, she handed me a folded piece of paper. I took the note from her, and she broke the silence before I started reading it. "God communicates to me in words, and I heard these words while praying for you." She was speaking fast, and although I heard what she said, I wondered if I had heard her correctly.

I glanced in Tony's direction to see if he was as dumbfounded as I was, but his blank expression didn't give his thoughts away. I looked at Uncle Jack for confirmation. He smiled but didn't say a word.

"God communicates to me in words, and I heard these words while praying for you."

Kim continued talking, "I don't hear God's voice out loud, but I hear a voice that is not my own in my mind. I think of them as God's whispers. I usually hear the words while I'm praying for someone, and I write them down as I hear them."

Although I was confused at the concept of God speaking to her, I decided not to question how that was possible. Instead, I blurted out what seemed like a really stupid question after it left my lips. "How do you know the words you heard are for me?" Even in my disbelief, I panicked at the thought that maybe I wasn't supposed to be the recipient of all of the whispers and promptings she had received since we started this wild ride. Tony was still silent, and I wished he would say something or ask a more intelligent question than the one I had just asked.

"Oh no, these words are for you," she assured me. "God makes it very clear who He is communicating about. Usually, I am praying for the person for whom I hear the words. Sometimes, God puts a person I haven't been thinking about on my mind, and when I pray for them, I will hear His words."

Speechless, I couldn't help but think, *Is she serious?* There was no reason she would make this up, but my conservative religious background made it difficult to believe. Tony got out of his chair to move closer to me so he could read the note. He was kneeling on one knee, leaning on the armrest. We read the note while Kim waited for our reaction.

There were several sentences, but I only focused on one: *"I will give you these children to raise up in Me."* I finished reading, folded the note, and put it in my pocket. Words failed me. *What does it mean?* My anxiety boiled down to plain disbelief, but I didn't want to let Kim see my doubt. We all stood up and I walked over and hugged her to break the awkward silence. I was feeling light headed when I whispered, "Let's talk about this later. We have a long drive home, and I need to absorb this when I'm not so tired." Tony also gave her a hug, but didn't say a word about the note.

It was a cool evening, and Tony and I put our jackets on before heading out. As we pulled out of the driveway, I said, "Wow, that was insane." After a few seconds of silence, I asked, "Do you think Kim is a nut?"

"No, I don't think she's crazy," he said. I was surprised that he seemed more humored by my reaction than to what had just transpired with Kim.

"Then you believe she hears the voice of God in her head?" I asked doubtfully. I nervously ran my hand through my hair, feeling anxiety about what had just happened *and* Tony's calm demeanor.

"I believe it is possible. Do you remember my friend, Betty, from New Mexico?" He didn't wait for me to answer. "She has the same gift of prophecy that Kim has. She was like a second mother to me when I was growing up, and I spent so much time with her that I got used to her unusual relationship with God."

"You never told me about her 'gift' from God," I said, fidgeting once again with my wedding ring.

> My desperation to be pregnant made me want to believe.

"It never came up, and it didn't seem important. Why does it matter anyway?" He sounded amused, and although it was dark in the car, I could see a smirk on his face.

"I guess it doesn't matter. I'm just surprised you never mentioned it." I added jokingly, "I probably would have thought she was a couple cards short of a full deck."

"That's why I didn't mention it," he said smiling.

All the way home, I struggled to wrap my head around the concept of prophecies in today's world. I believed in prophecies from biblical times, but couldn't shake the skepticism that they still exist today. It was like being in a twilight zone. Logic said, "No way," but my desperation to be pregnant made me want to believe.

My prayer that night was four simple words: *God, is it possible?*

Prophecies

I became a woman obsessed!

Early the next morning, Tony walked by my room and saw me purposefully clicking away on the computer as I began my research on *prophecy* on the Internet.

"What's up?" he asked.

"Nothing," I answered without looking away from my computer.

He wasn't convinced. He has always teased me for my obsessive behavior and the need for so many little "projects" in my life.

"Nothing?" he asked suspiciously.

I looked up at him and smiled. "Did you know there are over 81,000 listings on the Internet under 'Hearing God's Voice'?"

"Here we go again – another project for your obsession." He shook his head and murmured something else under his breath as he walked out of the room.

"Well, you asked," I yelled in his direction. "At least it keeps me busy!"

Many hours of research later, I had filled three binders with articles, and had four new books on order. The book that interested me the most was *Surprised by the Voice of God* by Jack Deere. It was a fascinating book on how God speaks today, through prophecies, dreams, and visions. What Kim referred to as words from God, he referred to as prophetic words coming from prophetically gifted people.

Deere discussed several ways in which God communicates with us, including visions, impressions, and one that he called the internal audible voice of God. This most accurately described the way Kim told me she hears Him. Deere wrote: "When God speaks to us in complete sentences in our minds, even though the vocabulary may be our own, the voice comes with an authority that causes us to recognize those sentences coming from God."

He also mentioned that it is not uncommon for God to speak to us through family, friends, and acquaintances, but cautioned that people can be hurt by misinterpretations.

After a lot of research, I was convinced that it is possible to experience God in a personal way.

I started to believe that prophecies do still exist. As to accuracy and interpretation of God's intentions through prophecies, I'm still not so sure. From my research, there are a lot of people taking action on what might be misinterpretation of God's whispers, but the revelation that God still whispers at all was exhilarating to me and came when I needed it the most. My days and eventually weeks of research helped me to process and have more confidence in Kim's whispers and visions.

The Implantation

God was closer than ever, but I was still very nervous about the journey ahead. The Friday after Thanksgiving, Kim had her eggs extracted. I wasn't feeling well that day, so I didn't meet her in Los Angeles at the clinic as we originally planned. Instead, she went with Aunt Carol and Uncle Jack to have the procedure done, and flew back home to her husband and four children the next day.

We were all excited to find out there were twenty eggs extracted, although several days later, we learned that not all were viable for implantation.

Tony and I were sitting in the doctor's office when we received the disappointing news. "The quality of the embryos was not as good as we hoped," the doctor said. He was a kind man who had been straightforward with us since the beginning. Through the process, he had been very patient with my questions and honest with his answers. "There was one embryo that we would give an 'A' rating, three considered 'Bs,' and three considered 'Cs.' The 'Cs' will definitely not become babies."

Although I wasn't visibly upset, I was sad there weren't more embryos. "So how many will we be implanting?" Tony asked. He didn't show much emotion, but I heard the disappointment in his voice.

"I would definitely recommend we implant all of them," he said with concern, "and perhaps you should consider a younger donor if there needs to be a 'next time.'"

Tony and I sat quietly for several seconds. I was upset that the doctor did not sound more confident and finally broke the silence with a question I knew Tony was wondering too, "What are the odds of us getting pregnant?"

"I would give you a 15-20% chance of getting pregnant with one baby, and less than three percent for having twins," he said as he closed our file.

"Okay, then let's implant all seven," I said, not allowing my disappointment to show. Tony and I both knew that successful or not, there would not be a "next time" for IVF.

I was depressed as we walked out of his office. "I know you are upset, but we still have seven chances to get pregnant," Tony said to break the silence.

"I know," I whispered, determined to hold it together.

"And don't forget that this has been a journey of faith, not odds and statistics," he added as we approached the car. I thought about what he said and knew he was right.

> I would give you a 15-20% chance of getting pregnant with one baby, and less than three percent for having twins.

"You're right. I'm not going to let this bum me out." When he opened my car door, I gave him a quick kiss on the cheek and slipped into my seat. By the time we got home, my depression had turned to nervous excitement. Our appointment for implantation was scheduled for a couple days later, and I was determined to get myself emotionally prepared.

The next few days flew by. Other than finishing a few loose ends at the office, I spent most of my time praying, listening to upbeat music, and reading. The morning of December 7th, which was the seventh anniversary of my first date with Tony, the doctor implanted seven embryos. The pregnancy test was scheduled ten days later on December 17th. I decided seven was our lucky number.

I was given a list of things to do (and not to do) to improve our odds of getting pregnant. One instruction was to lay flat and have very limited activity for three days. To be on the safe side, I laid flat for five days rather than three, only getting up to go to the bathroom, and I did very little for the five days prior to the appointment. It was truly the longest ten days of my life.

"In the dream, I saw two very strong heartbeats... and one very weak one."

I had planned to do all sorts of reading and catching up on paperwork for my business during my down time. Good intentions, but I was too anxious, excited, nervous, and terrified to be even a little productive. My family visited frequently and helped out with everything, so I was able to do nothing but rest.

On December 17th, Tony and I anxiously headed off to the fertility clinic to find out if we were pregnant. The past two months had been an emotional roller coaster. I called Kim on the way just to hear her voice. I knew she would calm my jitters.

"Kim, I'm feeling nervous." I glanced in the mirror as I was talking to Kim and winced at how disheveled I looked. I was so distracted before we left that I hadn't changed out of my black sweats, dried my hair, or put on makeup.

"Don't be," she sounded confident. "In the dream I had last night, I saw two very strong heartbeats on an ultrasound and one very weak one. I still feel the presence of a third child in your lives, but I don't know how to interpret that part of the dream."

"Okay," I said, not knowing how to respond. "I'm probably stressing for no good reason…"

She cut me short. "You are. Call me when the doctor tells you that you're pregnant. Love you." If she was nervous at all over the outcome, it was not in her voice. *But how can that be?* I briefly wondered if her confidence was all a facade, and the truth was that she was having a nervous breakdown that she didn't want me to hear.

At the clinic, they drew blood and told us it would be an hour before the doctor could give us results. It turned out to be *two* hours that felt more like three days. The confidence I had borrowed from Kim was fading, and I was rapidly becoming a wreck. While waiting, Tony and I went for a walk and stopped for a bagel and coffee. I was too nervous to eat with so much running through my mind.

Tony couldn't sleep the night before, so I know he was nervous, although I think he was stressed for different reasons than I. He desperately wanted a child, but he was also concerned about my mental and emotional well-being. If we didn't get pregnant, he had to handle his disappointment *and* mine.

As we walked, questions of faith consumed my thoughts. "My faith will be changed forever based on the outcome of this pregnancy test," I said. Tony didn't say anything. "If we are pregnant, it will all be good, but what if…"

He sensed I was starting to spiral in my thoughts and cut me off. "We will get through this together. Let's take it one step at a time. Right now, we need to trust in God's plan. We don't control anything else." He squeezed my hand, and we continued walking in silence.

I was testing God. *How much will my faith change based on the outcome of this day?*

We went back to the clinic after an hour and had to sit for another hour in the waiting room. The second hour was more stressful than the first. Doubt continued to consume me. I flipped through magazines without focusing on the stories. I paced to the water fountain and bathroom several times just to get up and move. Tony tried to distract me with tic-tac-toe, but after a couple games, I was up and pacing the floor again. It seemed like an eternity. And then…

"You are definitely pregnant!" I was expecting someone to take us to a room to get the results, but it was the doctor himself that came walking into the very large waiting room.

As he walked toward us, he said, "From the blood count, there are at least two babies and possibly three."

The doctor and a few people in the waiting room were thoroughly enjoying the moment, but neither Tony nor I could move or speak. After several seconds of silence, we began hugging and crying, and the doctor excused himself to give us the moment.

As soon as the tears subsided, we pulled out our phones and called everyone we knew, barely noticing that everyone in the waiting room was caught up in our joy.

There had been so many people praying for us, and the call list was long. From the waiting room, I called my mother, knowing she would alert the rest of my family who were all anxiously waiting for some news.

What an amazing day. What an amazing God.

Next, I called Kim, who laughed and cried and praised God for His goodness. We continued the calls to family and friends through lunch. Tony greeted everyone with, "Cappelli, party of five," while I corrected him with "party of four." The thought of triplets thrilled him, but I told him twins would be plenty. *What an amazing day. What an amazing God. What an amazing cell phone bill. Thank you, God!*

Cappelli, Party of Four

There was a lot of stress for me throughout the first twelve weeks because of the high rate of miscarriage. I tried to take it easy, working less and getting lots of rest, and began to relax a little more after the first trimester. Tony thoroughly enjoyed the pregnancy from the beginning and was involved with everything. He even gained weight with me. He would respond to all of my whims and cravings, and there would always be two of whatever I was asking for, one for me and one for him.

Thinking back, I had no true cravings to speak of. I was just hungry all the time and too tired to get up and make myself the chocolate sundae. So I would tell him it was a pregnancy craving, and he was happy to accommodate, both in making the sundae and in eating one with me. He was also good at cooking balanced meals for me to eat. I dislike most vegetables, so he watched me like a child until I ate all of them.

The pregnancy was a long one, especially since we knew we were pregnant after only ten days. At the first ultrasound, we found out we were having twins, and I was relieved, unlike my husband who seemed a little disappointed that we weren't having triplets.

One of the babies was getting more nutrition and the other was not growing at the normal rate.

We were both excited for their arrival, but wanted to revel in the nine-month journey. It delighted me to see Tony so involved, wanting to be a part of every aspect of the experience.

Before we knew the babies' genders, we called them "Pumpkin" and "Cruiser." Tony would sit for hours with the video camera, trying to record a kick or other movement. He would play songs on his guitar to them almost every night; and after we found out we were having a boy and a girl, he would play "Daisy Jane" by America to our daughter, and "Everybody's Trying to Be My Baby" by the Beatles to our son.

He rarely missed a doctor appointment and even wanted to be involved in the baby shower. We ended up having a shower for me, and a separate one for him. Mine was a combined baby shower with my sister, Julie's, since her son was born two months before our twins. About a month after that shower, a friend of Tony's had a "barbecue shower" for him and the guys. I was amazed how good the men (most of whom were over forty-five years old) were at baby-shower games. It was a sixty-year-old man who proudly displayed all of the diaper pins he won as he caught people crossing their legs during the evening.

Tony also enjoyed our Lamaze classes, and one in particular. All of the women were to expose their bellies so that a fetal monitor could be attached to their stomach to monitor the baby's heartbeat. Before exposing mine, I was checking out all the other women's stomachs, trying to decide if mine was going to be the largest one of the group.

I whispered to Tony, "Do you think my stomach is too big to expose?" He knew better than to answer that question honestly.

"Go for it." He sounded amused. "All the women seem to be consumed with their own bellies, so I doubt anyone will think twice about yours."

Finally deciding I was being vain and nobody would notice my huge stomach, I lifted my shirt so the instructor could monitor the heartbeats, and the laughter exploded. Horrified, I had no idea what could be so funny about my big belly.

In the chaos of the moment, I had forgotten that Tony had drawn a picture of a big Rawlings basketball on my belly earlier that morning. It was during basketball playoffs, and while getting in the spirit, he drew the basketball and wrote "official size and weight of the NBA" across my stomach. That was the last time I exposed my stomach to the group...or let Tony take a pen to it!

The Miracles Arrive

It was near the end of the pregnancy and I was anxious for delivery. Fetal monitoring and ultrasounds were happening three times a week. Feeling fat, swollen, and uncomfortable, I could barely fit into my maternity clothes or shoes.

It had also become apparent that one of the babies was getting more nutrition and the other was not growing at the normal rate. The doctors decided to take the babies by caesarian at thirty-seven weeks. So, on a very warm August 9th at 5:58 p.m., Nicolas arrived kicking and screaming. One minute later, Alexa joined him. Life would never be the same.

Due to some complications with the delivery, we were all on oxygen and in recovery for awhile. It was nearly eight hours before I could see them. The nurse had given me a photo to hold on to, but I was getting restless not being able to touch them.

Finally, at 2:00 a.m., two nurses came in my room, each of them holding a baby. I was asleep and Tony, in a chair next to my bed, was drifting in and out of sleep as well.

"Someone is here to see you," the nurse who was holding Alexa said to me. In an instant, I was awake and trying to sit up in the hospital bed, although the pain from the surgery quickly reminded me to move more slowly.

She gently put my daughter in my arms, and I could feel a tear stream down my face. I was overwhelmed with joy just looking at her. Alexa, who weighed 5 pounds, 9 ounces stared directly into my eyes with an irritated look that said, "Who are you?"

As I tenderly kissed her forehead, I whispered, "You look like you're going to be a handful. Is it just my imagination, or do you have attitude while only hours old?"

After a few minutes, a very proud daddy handed me Nicolas while I still cradled Alexa in my other arm. Nicolas was 4 pounds, 13 ounces, and so tiny and wiry that I was afraid I might break him. He was sound asleep.

Looking at both of our children in my arms at the same time, I said to Tony, "They are the most beautiful babies I have ever seen." I'm sure all mothers think that of their own babies.

I no longer question why the birth of my babies happened the way it did. *They are truly two of God's miracles, and I will celebrate every detail of how He brought them to us.*

What journey have you walked through that once seemed impossible, but in hindsight, you recognized the miracle of God walking alongside you each step of the way?

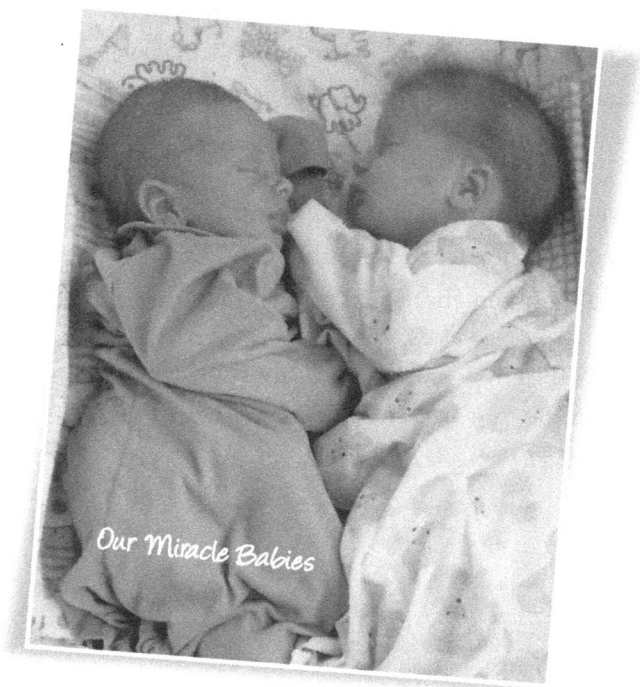

Our Miracle Babies

Chapter 3

That "Feeling"

"For we walk by faith, not by sight."

~ 2 Corinthians 5:7 NKJV ~

Four Months after Twins' Birth
January 1

Nicolas and Alexa were four months old, and we had just celebrated our first Christmas and New Year together. It was the first of January and a holiday weekend when I noticed something was wrong with one of our little miracles.

"She seems to be in good spirits. Why do you think something is wrong with her?" Tony asked as he took Alexa's temperature for the third time that morning. "Still no fever." He got up off of the floor where the babies were lying on a blanket. The sun was shining through our family room window, and they kept their little legs kicking at the ceiling, amused with the jingling sounds coming from the booties they were wearing.

"I don't know, but she doesn't seem herself. She has barely eaten for two days, and you know how she loves her food." I picked her up off the floor. "I think I'm going to take her to urgent care. I have this uneasy feeling that something is wrong, and I don't want to wait until tomorrow to take her to the doctor." I packed the diaper bag and headed off to an urgent-care facility with Alexa, fully expecting to return home with her in a couple of hours.

The facility was closed for the holiday with a sign directing me to the hospital, so I went there instead. The hospital waiting room was full of people, injured or sick, many with terrible coughs. I almost left thinking she would get sicker if I didn't. Yet that nagging feeling telling me I should stay persisted, so I waited.

"What is she here for?" The admitting nurse reached out and took Alexa from my arms. She was smiling, had no fever, and showed no visible signs of illness.

For a moment, I was questioning why I had brought her in. "She isn't eating and something seems a little off with her temperament." I thought about exaggerating some of her symptoms to justify the visit, but I stopped talking when I noticed the nurse's look of concern as she rolled Alexa from her backside to her front. She frowned a little and bent over to look closer at her face.

> Alexa was turning blue, and we were running down a hallway into a room with medical equipment and oxygen.

"Based on the color of her lips, she might be sicker than we think." Before I could comprehend her comment, Alexa was turning blue, and we were running down a hallway into a room with medical equipment and oxygen. My heart was racing and tears were rolling down my face. The nurse yelled something to the other medical personnel, but in my panic, I didn't compute what she had said. Within a couple of minutes, I was sitting on a hospital bed, holding an oxygen mask on my daughter who was oblivious to the chaos around her. She was batting at my hand that was holding her mask on but wasn't upset or crying like I was.

The first chance I had, I called Tony, who dropped Nicolas at my mother's house and met me at the hospital. Hours later, we learned she had the highly contagious disease known as Respiratory

Syncytial Virus (RSV). Due to her low birth weight, she was severely affected, and we spent a turbulent week in the hospital with Alexa in an oxygen tent.

When the week was over, we went home to a very sick Nicolas. Though not as sick as his sister, we still spent the entire month giving both of the kids breathing treatments. Several times a day, we had to hold a mask on each squirming child to administer the treatment into their mouth and nose. It was a battle to keep them still, and they would often cry during the fifteen-minute treatments.

It was such an exhausting month that it made me look very hard at another situation. Since the twins' birth, we were doing nothing to prevent another pregnancy. I knew the odds were small that I would get pregnant since Tony and I both have significant fertility issues.

But nothing is impossible. Somewhere in the back of my mind, I had a persistent feeling (similar to the one that had made me take Alexa to the hospital) that there might be another child in our near future. I struggled with the idea of another child, as I was already stretched to capacity with our twins and the insurance agency I owned.

Still Struggling
Early March

It was 1:30 in the morning, and I was tossing and turning, unable to sleep. "Tony, are you awake?"

Silence. I gave him a nudge. "Please wake up. We need to talk."

"What's wrong?" he mumbled. Before I could respond, he added, "and can't it wait until morning?"

"It can't wait. Please wake up. It's important."

He let out a groan as he rolled onto his back and waited for me to elaborate.

"What if we get pregnant?" I asked anxiously. Tired and stressed from another exhausting day with sick children, I was on the verge of tears.

> *I can't explain it, but I think we are going to get pregnant."*

"Huh?" he responded, clearly not thinking this was important enough to be talking about at 1:30 in the morning.

"You heard me. I know this doesn't seem critical to you, but I am freakin' out just thinking about it." I sat up straight in the bed.

With his eyes still shut, he calmly whispered, "Then don't think about it. We're not doing anything right now that will get you pregnant, so go back to sleep, and we can talk in the morning."

I turned away from him and started to cry. "We've been through this before," he said, sounding a little more sympathetic. "Please stop crying." He rolled over and put his arm around me.

"I can't explain it, but I think we are going to get pregnant." I was talking through my tears and sniffles, and Tony knew sleep was, unfortunately, not going to happen for either of us any time soon.

He sat up and tried to lighten my mood by saying, "Your eggs are no good, and my guys swim in circles and couldn't penetrate a good egg if you had one. More than one doctor has said so."

Not amused, I continued to sob. "I'm at my wit's end. I'm tired, cranky, and barely functioning from sleep deprivation – day after day, week after week. Nothing is getting easier for me. Another baby right now, with Nicolas and Alexa so young, will send me over the deep end!"

I was sure Tony had a humorous comment about my current state of mind without a third child, but he kept it to himself. He didn't say anything right away, but when he did, he spoke clearly and confidently.

"With odds so low of you getting pregnant, you must be feeling something that God has prompted." He paused briefly and added, "And if God wants us to have another child, then we should. Let God figure it out, and stop worrying about it." He put his arms around me again.

Laying in silence next to him, I wondered if he believed what he had just said, or if he just wanted to calm me down so he could go back to sleep. Regardless, it settled me down enough to pray: *God, I am very happy in this life you have given me with my two beautiful children, but if there is another child in the plans you have for us, then please Lord, give me a healthy baby, and the strength to handle another child.*

The Dream

A couple weeks later, around the middle of March, I had a dream. Remembering no specifics other than I was pregnant in the dream, I woke up feeling wonderful. Tony was feeding the babies when I came downstairs, excited to give him the good news.

"I'm good with it," I stated confidently.

"Okay," he said cautiously, completely clueless as to what the subject was.

"I had a dream I was pregnant, and I want you to know it's all good," I happily replied.

"Your mama's a nut," he said to Alexa, as he offered her another spoonful of something green. It was obvious that he did not think there was any chance of a baby in our future, but I didn't care. I knew I would be fine with or without another child.

> As I held the pregnancy test in my hand, I wasn't sure what I wanted to see.

Just then, Nicolas slammed his hand on a piece of banana, as if it was a bug needing to be squashed. Tony looked over at him smiling and said, "And you're a nut too, just like your mama." Nicolas gave him his toothless grin before he started sucking on the smashed banana stuck to his hand.

Taking a closer look at all of the food on the babies, the highchairs, and the floor, I interrupted him. "And who is the real nut here for feeding the kids bananas, peas, and whatever that orange stuff is in Alexa's hair this early in the morning. You're lucky they haven't spewed all over you."

Although we joked about the dream, it was a major turning point for me. For the first time in two months, I wasn't stressing over the idea of having another child. What I did not know at that time was that we were already pregnant and God was preparing me for the journey ahead.

Alexa & Sandy

Nicolas & Tony

Cappelli, Party of Five?
Late April

It was another six weeks before I found out I was pregnant. At lunch with my mother, I mentioned I was unusually hungry. "I haven't felt this kind of hunger since I was pregnant," I said as I looked over the menu.

Closing the menu, I noticed my mother looking at me with a blank stare. My small-framed Italian mother raised her eyebrows and asked, "Is it a possibility?" I hadn't given the idea of being pregnant much thought since Tony and I had discussed my dream.

"Hmm…" I said pausing a few seconds. "I don't think I am, but stranger things have happened to me." We were both silent for several more seconds. "Maybe we can pick up a pregnancy test on the way home." Considering how hungry I was when we sat down, I couldn't eat much after our conversation.

Hours later, as I held the pregnancy test in my hand, I wasn't sure what I wanted to see. It was a strange feeling. *How many times have I held negative pregnancy tests and wept over negative results? What if this is the first positive test?*

My expression must have said it all. Still holding the pregnancy test, I was trembling as I walked down the steps to where my mother was waiting for me. "My God," I whispered. "There is a baby growing inside of me."

My mom walked over and hugged me. Since the twins' birth, she had been over almost every day helping me care for them while Tony was at work, so this would affect her almost as much as me. Based on how much work the twins were for both of us, she must have been as nervous as I. But if she was, she didn't show it. We both sat on the steps, quiet at first, and then laughing and crying about the chaos we were in for having three kids under eighteen months old.

"We are in big trouble, Mom," I said looking in the direction of the twins.

Nicolas and Alexa, now eight months old, had fallen asleep in their car seats in the living room. We looked at them and knew peaceful moments like this would be even more rare once the new baby arrived.

I decided to call Tony at his office. We had been looking at new cars, and one of the cars we were considering was a Ford Mustang.

Trying to contain my excitement on the phone, I said, "Hon, I'm thinking the Mustang isn't a good choice after all."

He sounded preoccupied. "Oh, why is that?" I could hear him clicking away on his computer keyboard, so I knew I didn't have his full attention.

"I don't think we can fit *three* car seats in the back seat." There was dead silence on the phone. The clicking of the computer keyboard had also stopped. *I have his full attention now.*

His next words were a combination of disbelief and pure excitement. "Cappelli, party of five?!?"

"Yes, Cappelli party of *five*." Crying and laughing at the same time, I gave up trying to contain my emotions.

Tony was thrilled. And me. Well, I was both excited and a little overwhelmed at the idea of a baby on the way with my twins only eight months old. *Okay God, I left this one up to You, so You're going to need to see us through this.*

A few days later, Kim called and told me she had received a "word" (or whisper, as I have come to think of them) while praying for me.

Although prophecies are common to many Christians, they are still very new to me, and I felt cautious excitement.

But my cautious excitement became bewilderment as soon as I heard it:

"Fear not what is ahead of you for I have led you down this path." Why did she hear these words now? I'm feeling great and happy about the pregnancy. It sounded a little ominous, but I decided just to have faith in what was to come. *God will take care of us.*

When has a calling or challenge felt
ominous to you, yet you knew you
had no choice but to have faith
in God's plan?

Chapter 4

A Painful Decision

"So do not fear, for I am with you; do not be dismayed, for I am your God. I will strengthen you and help you; I will uphold you with my righteous right hand."

~ Isaiah 41:10 NIV ~

The Shocking Diagnosis
August 11

As I lay on the table, excitement rose inside of me. *I finally get to see my baby.* I couldn't wait to see all of its tiny features developing inside my womb.

"Let's see what's going on here," the ultrasound technician said as she began the procedure.

Believing this child was more God's will than even my own, I was not concerned about any problems, although I was eager to find out the gender. I didn't care what we were having, but I knew Tony was hoping for a boy. We already decided that if we were having a son, we would name him Steven, and if we were having a daughter, we would call her Brienna. Up to this point in the pregnancy, we had nicknamed the baby "StevieBrie."

The ultrasound technician was quiet for a couple of minutes before finally speaking. "Well, it looks like you are having a boy..." She didn't finish the sentence immediately, and sounded apprehensive about what she was seeing on the screen, "but there may be some complications."

My heart sank to the floor and panic took over. "What do you see?" I asked, tears already filling my eyes.

"I'm going to need you to talk to the doctor about his heart." She quickly finished the exam and left to retrieve the doctor after giving us some direction. "Go back to the waiting room, and he'll call you shortly with more information."

Tony and I didn't say much in the waiting room. We held hands in silence, although my heart and mind were racing the whole time. *What could be wrong? What did she see?* When the doctor called us in, we were told there was something wrong with the baby's heart, and he would be sending us to a specialist. He didn't want to give much information, but when I pressed him, he mentioned a heart defect that is sometimes associated with Down Syndrome. He reminded us that more tests were needed for an accurate diagnosis.

> *How could I possibly take care of a baby with a heart defect and two toddlers?*

I cried all the way home. The idea of there being something wrong with the baby growing inside of me was unbearable. *How could I possibly take care of a baby with a heart defect and two toddlers?* Tony was at a loss for words and didn't want to talk about the "maybes." He suggested we wait for facts instead of jumping to conclusions. I felt no comfort in his words and wondered how I was going to survive an entire week, waiting for the echocardiogram and the specialist.

God, why is this happening to our Steven?

God had blessed us in so many ways that I did not feel angry, and yet I felt betrayed. I had given the decision to have a child completely to God. A healthy baby and strength to handle him was all I asked. *Did You not hear me, Lord?* I sobbed, telling Him that I couldn't possibly handle this situation and prayed the echocardiogram would show it was all a mistake.

After a very stressful couple of days, I began to pray for peace. I had learned from the journey with my twins' birth that God is key to surviving my most challenging times. By the third day of waiting and prayer, I was feeling much more in control, knowing that if I prepared for the worst, I could handle anything. *God will be by my side and get me through.* By the fifth day, I had come to terms with possible doom.

On August 18th, the day of the echocardiogram, I was scared, but feeling stronger than I had felt all week. If the diagnosis was Down Syndrome with a heart defect, we would handle it. I had read that surgeries are usually successful for this type of heart defect, and we would just learn to adapt to the disability.

But this "worst-case scenario" had not even begun to prepare me for what we would hear.

"I'm concerned because I can only see two of the four chambers of the heart." The doctor performing the echocardiogram was friendly and had promised to talk us through the procedure. Tony, who had been comforting me by rubbing my leg, froze at the doctor's words.

There was a long silence before the doctor spoke again. "I see some other serious defects, and it might be better if I complete the exam and explain the results when I'm finished." From what little we had heard, and the tone of his voice, I knew the diagnosis would be worse than anything I had imagined.

I glanced at Tony, as he moved closer and grabbed my hand. Seeing the fear in my eyes, he squeezed it, and a tear slid down my face. And then I noticed how pale he looked.

"Honey, you look pale. You should sit down." But he refused to leave my side, and stood next to me until the exam was completed.

When the doctor was done, he and another male doctor consulted with us. They were both young, maybe mid-thirties, and they looked sad, almost uncomfortable, to me. It was as if they were leaning on each other to give us the bad news.

"Can this really be God's plan for Steven, the child He so deliberately created in me?"

The doctor who performed the procedure spoke, "It really can't get much worse than your son's heart condition. Not only does he have a severe case of Hypoplastic Left Heart (HLH), a very serious congenital heart defect, his condition is also complicated by several other major defects. There will be no chance of it correcting itself during pregnancy, and successful heart reconstruction after birth is highly unlikely due to the secondary defects."

Tony asked a couple of questions that the other doctor answered, but I heard nothing else; it was all white noise. My thoughts drifted far away. *Oh God, how can my baby be missing half of his heart?*

Tony and I were crushed. They left us alone for a few minutes to absorb the news. As soon as they left the room, Tony moved from his chair to embrace me. My arms around his neck, we cradled each other and wept for several minutes before pulling ourselves together enough to leave.

When we left the hospital, they gave us two pieces of information – one, to get a second opinion from Loma Linda Children's Hospital, and the second, to reinforce the possibility of aborting the pregnancy. I sensed from the doctor that terminating the pregnancy was the logical decision, and they urged us to do it soon due to the late stage of the pregnancy.

We were both in complete shock as we walked out the door. I was feeling weak and leaned on Tony as we made our way across the parking lot to our car.

"Can this really be God's plan for Steven, the child He so deliberately created in me?" Tony pulled me close and held me for a few minutes without saying anything.

My first call was to my mother so she could let my family know what had happened. My second call was to Kim. We have become close since the birth of my twins, and she always seems to have the words to comfort me in my darkest hours.

"It's really bad, Kim. The doctors don't expect him to make it."

Kim is not often at a loss for words, and I heard her ask through her tears, "What are your options?"

"We are going for a second opinion next week," I paused, knowing she would not agree with what I was about to say next. "They also gave me information to terminate the pregnancy and told me I should move quickly on it."

She was going to object, but I don't think she had the energy. "Sandy, you need to pray before you make any decision." There was another long pause, as if she was going to add something else, but instead whispered, "I'll call you later."

Later that night, the phone rang. Tony answered and told Kim I was sleeping, even though the reality was that I was too depressed to get to the phone. She urged him to put me on the line, so I finally agreed to hear what she had to say. "I've been praying and received another 'word' for you. I hope it will bring you and Tony some peace."

> "Know that I am with you and I am calling on you to do My will and not man's."

The message seemed hopeful but unclear, and Kim was unable to interpret it:

> *"Know that I am with you and I am calling on you to do My will and not man's."*

The words reverberated through me. *What does it mean?* I was fairly certain that God did not want us to terminate this pregnancy so I prayed that the visit to Loma Linda Children's Hospital for a second opinion would bring hope and shed some light. Falling to my knees, I cried out, *Oh God, please open a door for us to walk through. If surgeries can make our baby whole, give us a sign. Do not shut the door on Steven's life. Please.*

A Second Opinion
August 23

"What do you hope to hear?" Tony asked on our way to Loma Linda Children's Hospital.

It was a good question. There was no way the doctors could have missed seeing half a heart on an echocardiogram. He waited patiently for my answer. "I want to hear that there is a possibility that Steven might have a normal life."

"Do you have a definition of 'normal'?" There was no sarcasm in his voice, just deep sadness.

I had no immediate response, but drifted deep into my own thoughts. After several minutes of silence passed, I started to speak. "I would be willing to give everything I own, including our home and my business, to hear that some treatment – no matter how bad the odds for success are – will make him whole. I don't want our son in and out of hospitals his whole life, constantly in pain and fighting illness, and never experiencing the joy of life like Nicolas and Alexa. I just want so badly to hear that the problem will somehow be fixed, with no life-long complications." We pulled into the driveway of the hospital, and I gathered my referral papers *and* my emotions in preparation for the next few hours.

After another echocardiogram and meeting with the cardiologist at Loma Linda, the fatal diagnosis was confirmed. "Between his heart condition and the secondary problems with his system, there is no chance for recovery." The doctor discussed the painful options, none giving us hope for a normal life for Steven.

One procedure had a very low success rate and would require several open-heart surgeries. The concern was that the severity of damage to Steven's heart made him a poor candidate for a procedure that often ended in fatality under the best conditions. Based on initial results, doctors did not think this was a viable option because it involved reconstructing the existing heart, and Steven's heart was in really bad shape. The secondary major defect would severely complicate the reconstruction process or a heart transplant.

If we chose not to do the surgeries, Steven would only live for a few hours, maybe a few days.

Tony knew the answer to his question before asking, but asked anyway. "Do you think God is opening the door to treatment based on what we heard today?"

"No," I answered abruptly. "But the other choices are almost impossible to think about. How can I go the next four months feeling my child growing inside of me and then do nothing to try and save him once he is born?" Tears streamed down my face as I passionately poured my heart out. "Would this be a more compassionate answer to the hell he will be in if we try to give him life on earth? How can we possibly make this decision?"

Tony pulled off the freeway to try to console me, but I was spinning out of control. All rationality had disappeared. I was angry and hysterical, yelling, crying, and feeling utterly helpless over the situation.

Eventually, Tony took me home to grieve as I have never grieved before. I quickly slipped further into depression as the desperate, out-of-control feelings brought me closer to a complete breakdown…and further from God. I convinced myself I could never endure the next four months of life growing inside of me, knowing we would only be able to hold our son for a few hours.

Even Kim could not find the words to console me when I spoke with her that night. I sobbed hysterically, "Steven will be with God whether we abort now or He takes him after birth. So what is the purpose of enduring four months of heartache and grief when Steven will end up in God's hands either way?"

I knew she did not believe that God wanted us to end the pregnancy, but not being in our shoes made it difficult for her to convince me otherwise. I wanted the nightmare to be over. So much emotion, so much pain; it was unbearable. Steven kicked and kicked all night, hard and constantly, as if he knew his life hung in the balance.

Oh God, please take this child while I sleep.

I curled up in a corner of a very dark room, wanting desperately to give this decision to the Lord. But I already knew His answer. I knew in my heart that He wanted me to have His child. *But I do not believe I have the strength to carry out Your will.* If this was a test of faith, I was failing.

The phone jolted me from my thoughts. It was Kim's friend in Colorado, a person with whom I had never spoken before. She began telling me the story of her son who had died two years prior, after having lived for only ten days. My state of mind did not allow me to fully comprehend her story, but I felt her passion for God and for the child she had held for such a short time. She knew, without a doubt, that God had a purpose for her son.

But how does her situation apply to mine? I felt compassion for what she had been through, but I didn't know what it was supposed to mean to me. She had fought to save her child through surgeries, and in the end, God took her son to be with Him. I thought she was lucky. *She didn't have to make a decision.*

> Feeling great confusion, betrayal, and grief, I wrote a letter – the first of many – to God.

God could have waited for Steven to be born before exposing the heart defect, but instead, He was giving us a choice to end the journey or continue to have faith and walk with Him. In anger and pain, I pled, *God, please show me a way to have peace with Your will!*

A Reason
August 24

The next morning, I woke up knowing we would not end the pregnancy. God must have been at work while I slept, because the decision I struggled with so much the night before suddenly seemed very clear.

Walking into the kitchen where Tony was reading the paper, I whispered, "I want to give birth to Steven." My eyes were still puffy from crying, and I grabbed a tissue for the new rush of tears.

Tony reached out for my hand and pulled me over to him. Holding me on his lap, he looked into my eyes and whispered, "We will get through this together. I promise you, we will get through this." Tears streamed down his face.

"Mamamama" Alexa's sweet voice carried from her crib.

"I'll get her," Tony said. "Why don't you take a bath or a shower? Maybe you'll feel better."

"Or at least look and smell better," I managed a smile.

When I got to my room, I pulled out a piece of paper and pen and knelt on the floor by my bed. Feeling great confusion, betrayal, and grief, I wrote a letter – the first of many –to God.

> *Dear God,*
>
> *I have never actually written You a letter, but I am hoping to clear my head and to find peace. You have blessed me in so many ways. I can never lose faith or be truly angry with You, although I want You to know I am not happy. You have an agenda for me and for Steven, but isn't there another way? A child should be a blessing. But, God, I do not feel this is a blessing. I feel it is a sacrifice You are asking of me, and I will do it for You. My mind tells me You are God Almighty and I should not question Your motives, but my heart aches so much. Please take some of my pain away, and bring me peace. Give me something to hold on to – a reason for this sacrifice that I can comprehend.*

Later that morning, I was given new hope. I had just finished drying my hair when Tony walked in with a determined look on his face, and I knew he had something on his mind.

"Come sit next to me," he sat on the edge of our bed and patted the spot next to him. I slowly got up from my vanity chair and walked over to sit by him.

"What about donating Steven's organs?" he asked, before I had even sat down.

After several seconds of silence, I answered, "Maybe that's the reason for his life." I paused again. "If Steven could give life to other children, a part of him would live on forever." I took his hand and we discussed the concept of organ donation for some time.

The idea of donating Steven's organs brought light to a dark and unbearable situation. I could only hope that I would still see the light a few months from now.

Have you ever felt that God is asking you to make an unimaginable sacrifice to serve His will?

Chapter 5

A New Promise

"Be still and know that I am God."

~ Psalm 46:10 ~

Living with the Diagnosis
August 27

"Can you watch the kids for awhile?" I yelled over my shoulder as I hurried up the stairs.

I could hear squeals of delight from Nicolas and Alexa, and knew they were up to no good. They were in their highchairs, and Tony was reading the paper at the kitchen table. "Nicolas, don't do that with your bananas." Tony sounded more tired than amused. "Last time, they got stuck."

Nicolas loves entertaining his sister and, from the sound of Alexa's laughter, he was succeeding. I didn't turn back to see what he was up to, but I chuckled thinking about the fate of the banana.

"Sandy, don't be too long," Tony called out in my direction. I didn't answer as I closed the door behind me. With the door shut, the voices downstairs were barely audible. This rare silence is something I usually cherish, but today I wasn't looking for peace and quiet.

There was something important on my mind, and I couldn't get my laptop open fast enough to begin typing these words:

I heard a powerful church message this morning and I'm convinced God wants my story told. Although this spiritual ride began two years ago with the birth of our twins, the latest chapter of the tumultuous journey began a week ago when Tony and I went for a routine ultrasound to check the progress of my second pregnancy and found out that Steven has a fatal heart defect. I don't know how this story will end, but I know God wants me to write about the journey as it is revealed to me....so here it goes...

We have been blessed with so much love and support from everyone around us. And while the well wishes and prayers are wonderful, when all is said and done, Tony and I are the ones who have to live with this challenge every day.

Everyone thinks it is wonderful that we are going to donate Steven's organs, but it is still a long and painful four months away. People say we are strong, but I don't know how strong I am. I don't feel very strong every night when I wake up crying at 2 a.m.

I don't know how this story will end, but I know God wants me to write about the journey as it is revealed to me...so here it goes...

This morning, Tony and I talked in depth for the first time about the faith that is guiding us. We are both ready to sacrifice our baby if it is God's will because we know that Steven's conception was no accident. And God seems to be making it clear that He wants us to have Steven, if only to return him in a day or two.

What is the purpose in giving us a child for just a few days, Lord?

If God had asked me before I was pregnant to carry a child for Him, I would have said "yes" without hesitation. *So why is it so difficult to accept after the fact?*

"I need to find a way to cherish every kick, rather than feel the pain of this child we will never be able to raise," I said to Tony, as we were getting ready for church. "I want to have positive memories, and I'm going to find some way to do it." There was determination in my voice, but I still felt the need to look up from my vanity drawer and find Tony's eyes, and whatever acknowledgment or agreement he could give me.

Looking solemn, Tony nodded his head, but didn't say anything. I could see the concern in his eyes.

God, show us the grace to part with Steven when the time comes.

Sitting in church, I was consumed by my own thoughts and not paying much attention to the sermon. Tony was on my mind. *He has looked so sad lately.* I added him to my prayers, which are usually focused on the babies and me.

About halfway through the service, an elderly woman sitting next to me moved a little closer and asked, "Are you pregnant?" I nodded without saying anything.

"When are you due?" she whispered as the choir started another hymn.

"December."

"I will pray for you and your baby." She smiled sweetly.

"Thank you. We need all the prayers we can get." I had been feeling God's presence and the strength only He can give. I felt tears begin to well up inside of me and turned to Tony to quietly cry.

Several minutes passed before she spoke again. "Have I said something to upset you?"

"Not you." I paused, "My baby has a fatal heart condition." I could hardly say the sentence aloud as I realized I had not yet verbalized those words to anyone.

"Can we talk after the service for a few minutes?" she asked.

Seeing that she wanted to help, I nodded that we would talk later.

> "Sometimes bad things happen to good people and most of us never know the reason."

After the service, we spoke for a few minutes and she told me her name was Doleen. She reminded me that I can find hope through prayer, and she told me she would be praying for us. She didn't share any of her story, but I felt she had more to say and hoped we would talk again. It was comforting to know that she, along with so many others, would be praying for us.

Why?
August 28 a.m.

My emotions have been running high; I never know what kind of mood I will be in from one hour to the next. A good friend of mine, Terri, called this morning. We met more than fifteen years ago in college, and soon after, I was a bridesmaid in her wedding. Although we don't see each other as often as we used to, we still talk every week on the phone.

"I'm more accepting every day that God is in control of this situation and He will do with Steven as He pleases. I just want to know why the Lord is asking me to have a child that will die. I'm willing to do it, but it doesn't make sense to me. I can see no purpose in giving life to a child destined to die."

She said nothing while I finished my thought. "I'm not convinced that donating Steven's organs is His reason for taking my child, as much as it is my rationalization to deal with it all."

"Sometimes bad things happen to good people and most of us never know the reason," she said when I paused long enough for her to comment.

I didn't respond.

"Maybe it's to test our faith, strengthen our souls, reprioritize our lives – but the reality is that God doesn't always make it clear why things happen."

As I listened to her speak, knowing that everything she said was true, I found myself agitated at the idea that God may never answer my *"Why?"*

"Terri," I sighed, unable to hide the frustration in my voice. "I agree with some of what you say, but I still feel my situation is different. I didn't ask or pray for this child. With all of our fertility issues, I'm baffled as to how I even got pregnant." I was on a roll, and I could barely keep up with my thoughts. I didn't let her say much more in the ramble, but I think she knew I just needed to vent. I rambled on in an endless loop of unanswered questions before ending the call.

After my conversation with Terri, my depression, which had been looming large lately, worsened. God seemed to sense my need for intervention. Grace, my aunt, called about an hour later, and I gave her an earful too. Although she's my mother's sister, she is closer to my age, and we relate well. She is a good sounding board through this whole ordeal.

"Do you think God regrets choosing me for this task? I don't know if He knew just how high-maintenance I would be." She laughed with me, and I realized I am so grateful to her for understanding my twisted humor. It helps me through times like this, and she just lets me be me.

Please God, I know I should blindly trust without question, but I am human and I feel pain, and I really need to know. If You choose to take our Steven, why? Please give me that peace. If it is for other children through organ donation, open that door and make the path clear. I will accept your decision and give Steven back without ever asking why again. If it is for another reason, or if we should be taking a different path, God, make it clear. And as I have prayed so many times these past few weeks, give me the strength to get through this day.

I've suggested to God that if He reveals His plan a little quicker, He might not be so overloaded with prayers for Steven. Sometimes, I wonder if God gets annoyed with me for challenging His plan or offering suggestions. I've always thought I have a better way for everything, but I am beginning to realize deep down that I do believe God's plan is best. I only have to look at Nicolas and Alexa to know that.

Grace & Alexa

New Hope
August 28 p.m.

God may be answering. Earlier in the day, I spoke with Dr. Rodrigues (the doctor who delivered my twins) regarding the process of organ donation and the condition of Steven's organs based on last week's ultrasound. He told me he would have to check into it because a child with so many serious defects usually ends in miscarriage or early termination. He promised to call back today and he did, with more disappointing news.

"Your son's organs have limited value for organ transplantation," he said. "The baby must weigh a minimum of eight pounds, and the hospital will only want his corneas, and possibly some tissue.

I'm sorry I don't have better news for you." Heartbroken and sobbing uncontrollably, I hung up the phone.

About an hour after the call from my doctor, I got a call from my Uncle Jack. He and Aunt Carol, who are Kim's parents, are both ordained ministers practicing at a Christian nondenominational church. They are also my godparents and have been a wonderful support throughout the whole ordeal. Their faith in the Lord is as strong as any I've known.

Uncle Jack was clearly shaken as he spoke to me, but his words gave hope beyond my wildest imagination.

"Your mother called and was updating me on your situation." He paused and spoke a little more softly, "As she was talking to me, I was overcome by the presence of the Holy Spirit. This has only happened to me a few times, and each time God has provided a miraculous recovery for whomever I was praying for."

"What do you think it means for Steven's condition?" I asked.

Without hesitation, he answered, "I believe God's plans for Steven are bigger than we could possibly imagine. Maybe it is time to start praying for a miracle."

Not knowing what to say when he was finished, I said nothing. He sensed I was overloading and decided to give me time to digest our conversation.

"Let Tony know we are praying for all of you. I will give you a call a little later. Try to get some rest."

Far from Over
August 29

This afternoon, I went to the mall and spent a few brief minutes with Steven. My mom and niece were in line for a pretzel with my babies, and as I sat alone by a waterfall in the center of the mall, I realized that with all of my recent concerns for his health, I haven't spent much quality time thinking about him, my baby boy, growing inside of me.

As I sat watching the waterfall, I crossed my arms over my belly and gave him a big hug. "Steven," I whispered, "I promise to make the next few months the best I can for you."

He began kicking me as if he heard every word I was saying. "Buddy, I love you so much."

My moment with Steven was brief, interrupted by Nicolas yelling and shaking his fists at me from across the mall. I vowed to find more ways to celebrate Steven, no matter how long I have him.

Later in the day, I received an email from Uncle Jack that caused my emotions to soar.

Dear Sandy,

As I told you, the power of God during prayer has only come over me that strongly a few times. Each time, God demonstrated His power in some miraculous way. One of the more memorable times was about twenty years ago. A good friend of mine, Norma, and I were praying for a woman who had two large malignant tumors in her ovaries.

One of them was leaking fluid so badly that she could not get up out of bed and had to have her sheets changed several times a day. Before we left that day, the tumor had stopped leaking, and over the next two months, both tumors shrank and disappeared. I lost track of her recently, but a few years ago, she still had no recurrence of the cancer.

> "I think his healing will become noticeable in the near future. Get another test in about a month."

I am telling you this because, although this visitation of the Holy Spirit is rare, I have learned to appreciate when it is Him and not just my own spirit. What I believe the Lord told me yesterday is that Steven is going to be healed.

I think his healing will become noticeable in the near future. Get another test in about a month. I believe when you and Tony accepted God's will for Steven, and dedicated him to God's work, you tapped into the very power source of God's love. Steven will have a great impact on many people.

We love you,

Uncle Jack

My Aunt Carol also sent me a letter with her insight, directing me toward scriptures in the Bible that have already helped in coping with all that is happening. In her letter to me, she reminded me that God knows the plans He has for all of us, including Steven.

After reading their letters, I was so excited that I cried, and then so scared and exhausted that I felt numb. I wanted to believe what Uncle Jack said, but I was afraid – afraid to believe. Just when I resolved myself to the idea of letting Steven go, incredible hope has appeared.

Oh God, let this be Your promise for Steven. I want this child more than anything. But give me the strength to accept Your will. I fear that with this hope of a miracle, I may no longer be able to remain neutral to the outcome. Turning back will be difficult, so please Lord, make Your intentions clear. If I am to share this now with people I meet, please give me the words to say. If I am to continue to write this journal for others to read, please give me the words to write. And as always, give me the strength to get through this day.

Has there been a time in your life where you felt that God was speaking directly to you through someone else?

Chapter 6

Beginning to Let Go

"Let us be silent so that we may hear the whisper of God."

~ Author Unknown ~

Overwhelmed
September 2

Occasionally, my thoughts are jumbled; actually, my thoughts are often jumbled! Sometimes I write to clarify, sometimes I write to vent, sometimes I write to document. And a lot of times, these reasons are all mixed together.

In other difficult times, such as the infertility I experienced, I wrote about the research I had done. It helped. It all helped. I even created a manual four inches thick on every subject regarding my medical condition and fertility options. I think I intimidated, or at least annoyed, a couple of the many doctors we saw through that experience.

Mentally shutting down was all I could do as the doctors at Pomona Valley and Loma Linda Hospitals tried to put into words a very complicated situation. What I clearly remember from the initial diagnosis was one of the doctors saying that Steven has half a heart, with severe problems in the half of a heart that he does have.

Coming home from the hospital, I searched desperately on the Internet for information that would make me feel better. Research and knowledge are my key to sanity (or insanity, if you ask my husband) when dealing with challenging issues. But this situation is different. I am overwhelmed. Steven's heart condition is so bad that there is no point in doing research. I have some of the technical terms associated with the defect, yet there are many more that I can't even comprehend. I don't even know the name, if it has a specific name, of the secondary heart defect the doctors have referred to.

Hope lost, I turned off my computer. All I had left was prayer, and so I prayed myself to sleep. And the next day when I woke up with no answers, the overwhelming cycle repeated.

It has been over two weeks since the diagnosis, and still I sit here writing, unclear of my destination. Although writing usually helps with my anxiety, there are days when even my writing causes me stress. I wonder why I feel compelled to write and find myself asking endless questions. *Am I writing for me, for God, or for others to read?* My thoughts are a whirlwind. *Does anything I write make sense? Is this a journey of faith, of hope, or of promise? Is it about a mother's love, a miraculous healing, or a mother's grief?*

Is it about a mother's love, a miraculous healing, or a mother's grief?

Yesterday, I walked into the kitchen where Tony was reading a magazine while the kids were eating breakfast. Glancing at some pages of my manuscript that were left on the table, I picked them up and asked, "Why do you think I'm spending so much time writing about my crazy life each week?"

Tony ignored my question, but I looked up to see Alexa smiling as if she understood my crazy-life comment. She was well into her Cheerios with pieces of banana mashed into her tray while other chunks of it were matted into her reddish-brown hair. Nicolas was so absorbed with removing every remaining Cheerio from his tray and tossing it to the floor that he never even looked up when I walked in.

"I guess Daddy doesn't have an opinion," I said to the kids. "… which is rare," I added under my breath.

"Hmm," was all I heard from Tony. He was disinterested in my question and didn't look up from the magazine he was reading.

Even without his full attention, I continued on. "After a week of writing, I still feel compelled to write, but why? When I believed God wanted me to write, I also figured He would communicate to me what to say."

> "Even I question my own sanity at times like this."

Tony must have sensed I was going off on one of my emotional tangents. He closed the magazine and gave me a look that told me he was amused with my dilemma, but would at least give my amusing dilemma his full attention. He waited patiently for me to finish.

"So a writing fool I have been. Page after page after page. But after a week of writing, I peruse the pages of my efforts and can't help but wonder why. I do not see any poetic words of wisdom that God may have planted in my head. I read a lot of the pain, confusion, and tests of faith that most people would not dare verbalize, let alone put in writing. Who questions God's plan or puts 'Dear God' letters in writing? Even I question my own sanity at times like this."

He walked across the kitchen for another cup of coffee and murmured something under his breath as he pulled a Cheerio from between his toes. "Maybe you can help others going through challenging times." Taking a sip of coffee, he looked up at me with confidence that his words had solved my problem.

I didn't agree with him and found it even more annoying that he could think my dilemma would be so easily resolved. "I don't see how sharing this journey with all of my flaws, emotional ups and downs, and confusion can help others."

Tony chuckled. "You are obsessing, as usual. Just write. It occupies your time and gives you hope."

Not amused at his comments, I stood up and walked abruptly out of the room, leaving him with the babies and their bananas. This time, I muttered below my breath, "Husbands can be so irritating."

The Life I Planned
September 5

"Oh Steven, you sure have been busy this morning," I whispered as I kissed my hand and rubbed it over my stomach. "First the hiccups and now all the kicking. Go ahead, buddy, kick away!"

Holding true to my word and cherishing every one of those kicks, I pray daily for the strength to get through – one day at a time. Most of the time, I am at peace with my situation, but sometimes fear seizes me. Today was one of those days.

One of the most difficult things I am dealing with is not being able to plan. I've always had a plan – for the day, for the year, for my life. Oh, how I wish we could have a plan for Steven! *Should we set up the nursery for him? Should we start working on his scrapbook? Should we buy a van because three car seats won't fit in our vehicles?* I want desperately to plan for Steven, but I'm too scared to do it.

Our life is like a twister, emotions whirling in all directions, emotional debris flying everywhere. Fear creeps in like smoke under the door, but my God, who always makes His presence known just when I need Him, strengthens me.

Forgive me, Lord, for being scared. I have been such a planner my whole life, and this walk of faith is so challenging. Show me how to let go of the control I so desire, and walk this journey with You on faith alone. Right now, I believe Your plan is to heal Steven. But what if this is not your plan? Could there be hope and promise in the death of a child?

Watching Nicolas play in his Superman overalls today, I realized how badly I want to see Steven in those same overalls. I want to hold him and hug him and listen to him laugh. I want to wipe the peanut butter and jelly out of his ears, and watch him blow raspberries at me between bites of banana. I want to see his ear-to-ear grin as his daddy flies him around the room like Superman, and I want to wipe away his tears when his sister steals his pacifier.

I want a perfect day, just like today, with my Steven.

Moving Forward
September 8

I am so tired these days, and the physical pain seems to be getting worse as the pregnancy progresses. The scar tissue is being stretched, and it is too soon after my C-Section to have all of this stretching and weight placed on my belly.

Last week, I bent over a few too many times and could not walk for nearly a day. What concerns me most is that I still have three months to go, and the pain seems to be increasing with every week that passes. With my business and the twins, bed rest isn't an option. The combination of emotion and constant pain is wearing me down. When I ask God for strength to get through the day, I'll need to ask for physical strength too.

For a baby with a weak heart, Steven sure has strong legs. He's kicking relentlessly these days. And I love it! I want to feel him, talk to him, and talk about him more than ever. Sadly, a lot of people are uncomfortable and don't know what to say, so they say nothing. This hurts even more. I want people to acknowledge and remember Steven, regardless of how long he lives. *I have made the decision to celebrate his life however long he is to be with us.*

"He will not let me crash, whatever Steven's fate."

I tried to schedule an ultrasound at my last doctor's appointment, just to see him, but it wasn't to be. The technician showed no compassion as she denied my unusual request. She told me I would need a doctor's request and a separate appointment, and that my insurance would not cover it unless it was medically necessary. *I just want one more chance to see his tiny arms and hands, the curve of his nose and lips, and those strong little legs that keep kicking me awake every morning at 4:00 a.m.* Looking at the pictures from the last ultrasound helps me feel a little closer to my son. *Will he look like me?*

This afternoon, I was talking with my assistant who has worked for me for over ten years. She is several years younger than me, and has really stepped up to manage my agency during this turbulent time. Her reaction was typical. "What if..." she paused before finishing the sentence, "What if the miracle doesn't happen?" Like so many others, she thinks I'm going to have a meltdown if my prayer isn't answered my way.

"I don't really know. I can only hope God will get me through." As I spoke with her, I realized how far I have come from just a few weeks ago. "As stressful as it will be, I will find strength in God. The one thing I know with 100% certainty is that He has not taken me this far to drop me on my head. At times when I feel weak, I may question my own strength, but I never question His. He will not let me crash, whatever Steven's fate."

Be Silent
September 10

On my way into church this morning, I saw Doleen. She had a hug for me and asked, "How is Steven Joseph doing?" Hearing his name put a big smile on my face.

The sermon touched on the many paths God opens up for us throughout our lives. *So why has God chosen this particular path for me?* This experience is testing everything I've got. Following God's plan is the hardest thing I've ever done. I know I need to listen and wait, but I am so impatient.

A plaque that I recently hung in my bedroom reminds me of this every day: "Let us be silent so that we may hear the whisper of God." Even when God is quiet, I know He is with me, and I need to keep praying for His guidance. I have to remind myself that this is about God's plan, not my wants and wishes. Interestingly, I feel more peace when I "let go and let God." *So why is it a constant battle?*

When we first found out there was a problem with Steven's heart, I prayed it was a mistake. Deep down I knew it was not, but I also knew that God is Almighty and has the power to change things. I begged and pleaded and offered Him everything I had to give me a healthy Steven. But this was my wish, not necessarily God's will.

Day after day, I found little peace in spite of desperate prayers. Eventually, I began to pray for peace and the strength to get through whatever awaited me. I had no idea of the magnitude of Steven's diagnosis or what God would slowly reveal to us. Admittedly, it is much more difficult to accept God's will when the life of our child is at stake.

Oh God, will I have the strength to surrender to Your will as we get closer to delivery?

A Most Important Relationship

One of life's most precious gifts are the relationships that shape our lives. I really enjoy all of the new people I have met since Steven's diagnosis – the "Doleens" of my life. Relationships are what bring me the most happiness.

Money and the things money can buy are also good, but the people in my life make the real difference. My husband, my babies, my family, and friends; my staff, business associates, and even all of the one-time acquaintances I have met. I cherish the feelings I have for Nicolas and Alexa, the bond that is developing with Steven, and the relationship that I have with my own mother.

Less than two hours ago, I was sitting on the couch, working on this journal. My feet were elevated due to swelling, and I was trying to rest while putting into words how special my mother is. It was such a peaceful moment, reflecting on my amazing mother. And then I smelled the scent of baby poop in the air - a really strong scent! My kids were playing about ten feet away in my gated, baby-proofed family room. I was listening to their delightful chatter while engrossed in my writing, but decided I had to investigate the strong smell.

As I approached the gate, which was visible from where I was sitting, I was horrified. Had I been paying attention, I wouldn't be faced with baby poop smeared all over the carpet, walls, toys, gate, and air conditioner vent. Nicolas had no diaper on and the kids were more brown than white, kind of like gingerbread babies.

Certainly, Alexa was the brains of the operation and helped Nicolas take off his diaper. After all, wasn't it her duty to share her newest found skill with her brother? She learned how to take hers off last week and is not allowed to play in just a diaper anymore. I'm guessing she decided to teach Nicolas and, from the looks of things, he was an excellent student!

Barely able to walk or bend over to clean up the mess, I knew there was no way I could carry two stinky thirteen-month-old babies upstairs to the bathtub. Crying from mental exhaustion, I picked up the phone and started dialing.

"Mom, I need you here quickly," I said, wiping the tears from my face.

"I'll be right there. Are you all okay?"

I could hear the concern in her voice. "Yeah, we are all okay."

While searching for words to describe what had happened, she cut me off. "I'm already heading for the door. See you in a few minutes."

Crying from mental exhaustion, I picked up the phone and started dialing.

As I hung up the phone, both kids were watching me as I limped toward the kitchen cabinet. I pulled my camera off the shelf and headed back to them for a closer shot. Nicolas was clueless and smiling his toothless grin, but Alexa knew I wasn't happy with the situation. Through the tears, I was thinking to myself, *This isn't the least bit funny now, but I know it will be funny someday.*

Before I had finished taking the pictures, my mom came running in the house. When she got to the gate and saw me sitting on one side of the gate and the kids smeared in poop on the other side, she stopped and stared in disbelief.

"Oh my," was all she said before she began laughing, as she scooped up a stinky kid and headed up the stairs to the tub. Within an hour, my kids, carpets, walls, toys, gates, and air conditioning vents had all been scrubbed and were poop-free.

That's my mother. Always around, always helping out, and always making things better. Throughout my whole life, she has supported me and all of my endeavors. She was never too loud or controlling, just always nearby. No way could I have handled all of the challenges my crazy life has encountered these past couple of years without her. She is one of God's greatest gifts to me, and I love her with all of my heart. I can only pray that I will influence my children's lives in the positive way my mother has influenced mine.

Have you ever been
forced to let go and let God,
and witnessed the support
He gives when you do so?

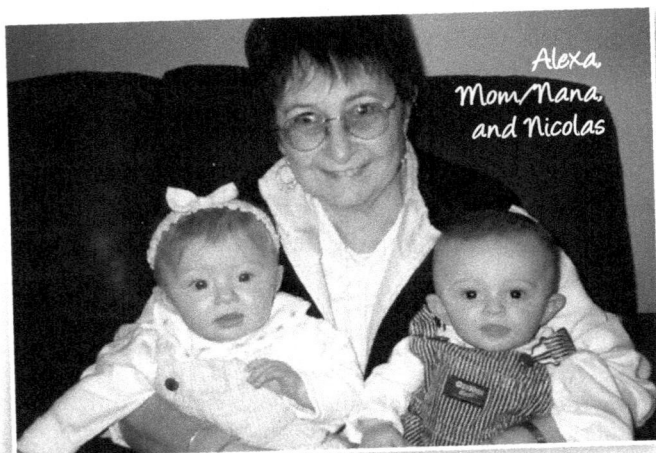

Alexa,
Mom/Nana,
and Nicolas

Chapter 7

I Want to Believe and Trust

"Trust in the Lord with
all your heart, and lean not on
your own understanding;
In all your ways acknowledge Him,
and He shall direct your paths."

~ Proverbs 3:5-6 NKJV ~

Seeking More Answers
September 14

I called Uncle Jack today and asked him a lot of questions about prophecies and what his opinion is of prophets in today's world. Still confused about promptings from God, I thought he might shed some light on the subject, and maybe help me understand Kim's prophecies. He told me he would put his thoughts in writing, and I received this email a few hours later:

Dear Sandy,

Kim is exercising the gift of the Holy Spirit called Prophecy, as described in 1 Corinthians, Chapters 12 and 14. In this gift, the Holy Spirit gives the receiver thoughts, pictures, visions, and/or words that form in the mind.

The words given to Kim are being directly expressed, which is different from when I receive a word, which almost always comes as an understanding of a message that I need to interpret. They are thoughts put into Kim by the Holy Spirit, but because they come through a human speaker, they always need testing to be sure the speaker has not changed them in some way.

There are three primary tests. Do the words agree with Scripture? Do the words edify or encourage the audience? Is the speaker, both in personal character and by experience, a proven vessel of God's message? Having observed Kim's messages over a long period, I can testify to the first question. They have always met the test of

Scripture. The other two, you have to judge for yourself.

Let me add some thoughts on Steven. I had an experience of God's presence when I was talking to your mom, where the Holy Spirit came upon me, quite unmistakably. I immediately had a sensing that His presence was related to Steven's troubles, and I interpreted His message as being that Steven would be healed. I was heavily moved by the Spirit until I verbalized Steven's healing, and then I received a strong sense of peace. I was sure enough of the experience that I assumed that the doctors would see an immediate change in Steven's situation. However, that was my idea and my desire. God's ways are above our ways, and He has His own timing and plans.

"The answer is no and yes."

The next question is whether it is possible for Kim and I to both be wrong in our experiences and interpretations. The answer is no and yes. It is highly unlikely we have mistaken our experiences, but being human, we could have misinterpreted the meaning. That is where faith comes in. Abraham was visited by an angel and still had trouble believing he was going to have a son. And he is held up as Scripture's model of faith. I know I don't claim to be in that class, and I suspect Kim would agree with me. At this point, God has given us multiple indications of His plan, but He never gives an ironclad guarantee. He always wants us to participate with prayer and faith.

He also wants the prayers of the whole family behind this, because this baby is more than a gift to just you and Tony. He is a gift to all of us, just as the twins have brought us all together in preparation for this. Sorry for the long-winded response, but Steven has been much on my mind these past days.

Love you,

U. Jack

Are We Listening, Lord?
September 15

I have become really intrigued by words and prophecies from God, and have been thinking a lot lately on ways that God communicates with us. *So why aren't more people able to experience this kind of communication with Him? Are we not listening to Him?*

My biggest fear is that I might be wrong. *What if it's just a crazy voice or thought in my hormonal head that I think is God's prompting?* I doubt I'm the only one who has brushed an experience off as coincidence, luck, or fate, instead of recognizing it as the voice of the Lord.

Grace and I were discussing the wonderment of prophets in today's world, but decided maybe there is a reason we all don't have dreams, visions, or clearly hear God's words. I did have the dream of being pregnant at the time of Steven's conception, but I could not remember a single detail of the dream. I just woke up with a wonderful feeling of being pregnant. I did not pray for that dream; it just happened. In fact, it seems like the times I have asked God to come to me in a dream, I end up dreaming about monkeys or something equally irrelevant.

It would be nice to clearly hear words from God to help me through my own crisis, but I would not want the responsibility of receiving His words for other people. I have come to depend on Kim so much during the difficult times. *But how can she possibly know God's true intentions for Steven?* It is only her interpretation of what God communicates to her.

Barely able to keep my own head above water, I know I can't handle other people turning to me for answers during their darkest hours. Perhaps it is because God knows my strengths and weaknesses. Maybe that is why my dreams are about monkeys.

> *But how can she possibly know God's true intentions for Steven?*

Control
October 1

God is on my mind all the time these days, and researching how He communicates with us makes me feel closer to Him. He becomes more real to me with each week that passes, and I find myself thinking about Him as often as I think about Steven every day. This brings me peace.

One of the concepts I read about focused on control and learning to let go. It really hit home. Letting go of control is one of the hardest things for me to do. From the lack of control over this pregnancy and Steven's fate to less control in my business, it is very difficult for me to do. Since having the twins, I decided to spend more time at home, which has made me feel less in control of my business. When I'm at home, I feel the babies are in the best care, but I sometimes worry about details in the business. *Are my customers being cared for? Are claims being processed? Are we writing any new policies? Will I be able to pay all of the bills?*

I continue to pray for help with my control issues. Lately, I involve God in a lot more of my daily decisions. I used to think I shouldn't involve God except on pivotal decisions that would dramatically influence my life. I didn't want to bother Him with the trivial things so that He would give my major dilemmas His full attention. Now my thinking is somewhere in the middle as I seek some balance.

From concerns about finances to health issues, I'm trying to control less and trust more. Before Steven's diagnosis, I was consumed with worry about money, while now I seldom think about it. We seem to get through each month, which is all that matters to me right now. I will worry about the future when the present isn't so chaotic. It is a matter of priorities, and there is so much going on in my life that money has been booted from the #1 position. My priorities now look more like this:

- Steven's condition and all of the related doctor appointments
- my new relationship with God
- gestational diabetes, diet, and glucose testing

- whether the pain in my side will keep me from walking or require total bed rest

- the constant demands of 13-month-old twins, which eliminates the option of total bed rest

- the magnitude of this pregnancy and whether we will be celebrating a true miracle of physical healing, or burying our son in December

- major changes happening in my business

- my husband's career move

- this book

- health concerns for my aging father-in-law and two other family members

- my mental state from all of the stress in my life

- and, oh yeah, money…

Humor is as helpful as prayer at times like this.

Wow. It looks bleak when I list them all out. There was a time when any one of these things would have consumed me. But somehow, I am dealing with my crazy life. I have magnified the blessings in my life – my babies, husband, family, staff, all of the people praying for Steven and me, and most of all, God.

In the same way I am magnifying my blessings, I'm trying to minimize the strife in my life. I don't dwell on difficult situations for too long, and I try to never think about all of them at once! Just listing them all out in the previous paragraph has my heart beating faster than normal.

Focusing on one day at a time, one problem at a time, and lots of prayers seem to be working for now. Either that, or it is the lull before the storm, and one more straw will break this pregnant woman's back and send her straight to the funny farm. If my life becomes any more challenging, a funny farm may be just the vacation I need. At least it sounds like a happy place to visit.

Fortunately, I can still find humor in my life. Humor is as helpful as prayer at times like this.

Changing Priorities
October 3

I've been consumed with Nicolas and Alexa lately. When I am overwhelmed, I turn to them for comfort. They help me to refocus my priorities on what is truly important in life, as it is hard to feel depressed when I see their bright little faces. A couple of days ago, Alexa picked flowers for me from our garden. *Being a mom is wonderful.* And yesterday, while driving in the car, I looked in my rear-view mirror to see them sitting in their car seats, stretching their arms out so they could hold hands with each other. *They are such great buddies.* Moments like these are precious to me.

I never realized how much my life and priorities would change once I had the twins. I really believe the fertility problems I experienced helped me to be a better mom and appreciate the blessings they truly are in my life. *I never thought I could love so deeply. I never thought I would put my business on hold so I could spend more time watching my babies grow.* I am learning to lean on others and let go of my pursuit of perfection. I think lowering my expectations in areas such as my business has helped tremendously.

I wanted to see my babies' first smiles, see them take their first steps, and hear them say their first words. I also never thought I would be willing to trade everything I own – my business, my home, and my money – to make my unborn child healthy. *Where did the selfish me go? I hardly recognize myself anymore.*

Nicolas and Alexa are such happy babies; I believe this is just one of the benefits of putting my business on hold to make them my priority. I wonder what their personalities will be in a few years. They are growing up so fast, and changing every day, from the foods that they eat to the confidence in their walk. They are imitating everything I do. Alexa insists on brushing her own hair, and unfortunately Nicolas' too. He hates it and usually runs for cover whenever she shows up with the hairbrush. They love all of the new games we make up and the songs we sing together. Their personalities are growing, and they are developing into such interesting little people.

Nicolas loves to be pushed around on his Big Wheels while Alexa is into chatting on the telephone and wearing things on her head. It started about a month ago when I put a pair of her panties on her head while folding laundry. She immediately began walking around with a big grin, thinking she looked beautiful. Laughing hysterically, I looked over at Nicolas who was giving her a look that said, "You have no idea how stupid you look." Since then, she has put everything from hats to baskets to diapers (clean ones, fortunately) on her head. For the past few days, the spaghetti strainer has her strutting around like a beauty queen.

It is interesting to see how different they are too. Nicolas is slightly smaller, has olive skin, brown curly hair, brown eyes, and dimples just like his daddy. Alexa was born with red hair that is now a thick mane of wavy light brown hair with just a hint of red. She has fair skin, chubby cheeks, and big beautiful blue eyes. My children look nothing and act nothing alike. Nicolas is a child of few words with a very sweet temperament, while Alexa chatters all day long and already has a strong will of her own. *I knew it the moment I looked into her eyes.*

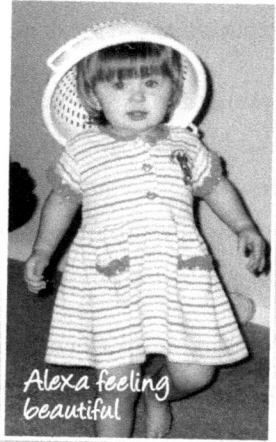

Alexa feeling beautiful

What surprises me even more than how different they are, is how gender-oriented they already are at thirteen months. *What makes Nicolas like to race around like a daredevil, while Alexa prefers to take in all of the sights around her? Why does Alexa prance around with things on her head and love to put on new clothes?* Any clothes will do, but frilly ones with her patent leather shoes seem to please her most. Nicolas, on the other hand, could care less about clothes, and would play in a diaper all day if it were up to him.

Why is it that Nicolas runs from me when I try to brush a little of my makeup on him, while Alexa comes running to me and eagerly awaits her turn? Up to this point, I have treated them the same with no special gender toys, and already, Alexa is all girl and Nicolas is all boy.

Now What?
October 9

Yesterday's OB/Gynecologist doctor appointment was not as bad as the previous appointment, when I found out that I had gestational diabetes, but it was still depressing. The doctor asked if I would be donating Steven's corneas. I told him that is our plan, if Steven doesn't need them. *That was an awkward moment.*

Doctors that I trust are telling me Steven will die. They give me no hope that the situation can change. I leave with no hope, because they give me nothing to hang on to. Then I think about God, His signs of hope and healing regarding Steven, and His amazing power; and suddenly, my hope is restored. *If God wants Steven to live, he will live.*

The echocardiogram scheduled for October 18th is only a week and a half away. I have tried not to think about it for fear the anxiety will consume me. Uncle Jack seems to think we will see God's healing powers when we go. *I hope so. I'm still too afraid to set up the nursery or buy the van. Maybe after that appointment, I will have the confidence to plan for Steven.*

Still devouring books these days, I find the right ones continue to keep me focused and help me find peace with my turbulent life. The one I have been reading this week is called *IF LIFE is a GAME, THESE are the RULES* by Cherie Carter-Scott, Ph.D. It revolves around ten rules for being human. While sitting in the waiting room of the diabetes clinic this morning, I was reading about a concept revolving around the idea that every person creates his or her reality. The challenge of this rule is to create and own our own reality. The first moment we are able to do this is an awakening of sorts, since it means the demise of our unconscious life.

> *I would rather stay in a place of unknowing with no concerns of disappointing God.*

As I read an example of the author's own life experience, I found something disturbing, yet familiar about what she was saying. Before I could pinpoint the "what" and "why" of my uneasy feelings, I was called in to see the technician at the diabetes clinic. We began talking about my upcoming week, and I mentioned my nervous anticipation over my echocardiogram scheduled on the eighteenth. Even though I hardly know her, I've trusted her enough to share Steven's story with her.

I felt myself becoming emotional, as my words began to express what was disturbing me before I met with her. What is so unsettling to me is that in my quest for a closer relationship with God, I'm also developing a new fear of Him. He has become so real to me; He is everywhere in my life. He knows me better than anyone else does. He is no longer vague to me. I know firsthand that "God is." These are all wonderful things that should bring me joy as the relationship I desperately seek develops.

What frightens me is that with all of my new knowledge, I'm sensing the demise of my own unconscious life. There are times like today that I would rather stay in a place of unknowing with no concerns of disappointing God.

There was a time, not long ago, when I thought there would be nothing greater than for me to recognize the voice of God. And now, a short time later, I'm feeling stressed by it all. If I clearly understand what He wants of me, what my true path or destiny is, I will need to carry out His will and not necessarily my own.

I remember vividly the stress that I felt the night of August 23rd when I was trying to decide whether to terminate the pregnancy. Whether it was Kim's influence, her friend's story about her child who had died, or God speaking directly to my heart, by morning I knew I would not end the pregnancy. Without a doubt, God wanted me to have this child "who was destined to die." It made no sense, but I knew it was His will, and I needed to carry it out.

God brought me peace with His will, but the clarity of what He wanted me to do was accompanied by fear – and still is. Now, in my new reality that is developing, I know that He is in control. *If I decide to follow my will and not His, I will know I have failed Him.*

My Fear of the Lord
October 10

I was folding clothes today while the babies were napping when Tony walked in from running some errands. He offered me a sip of his soda and asked how my day was going. I usually have the television or music on while I do chores, so it was unusual that I didn't, and to have the house so quiet. We began discussing my recent feelings and concerns that I've had since finishing the book on rules for life. He could not grasp the stress I was feeling, so I dug deeper for an explanation.

"It involves control and the concern that I will disappoint God if I don't like His plan for me. This is hard for me to wrap my own mind around, and explaining it to you is even harder." He could hear the frustration in my voice.

"Maybe you are not so much afraid of God as you are of the unknown."

> Now I feel there is something certain in my future that He has planned for me. It is as if He is preparing me in these journeys of faith involving my children for something even bigger.

"I hope you're right. I don't want to be afraid of God. I'm just having trouble defining what is causing these stressful feelings. It is a huge concept, and pinpointing exactly what is bothering me is difficult." Stopping for a minute to gather my thoughts, I slowly continued, "When I break it down, I guess it doesn't bring me so much fear. I want God in my life. I know His plan is better than my plan. So why do I fear what God may ask of me in the future?"

"You need to think a little less and trust a little more," Tony said in a matter-of-fact tone. Tony seldom shares about his faith in God, and up until now, neither have I. Even though we go to church together, we don't pray together. *I wish it were easier for us to share our faith with each other. We've both made some huge strides in our spiritual growth since the twin's birth, but we still have a long way to go.*

Even knowing Tony's comments made sense, they did not relieve my stress. Until now I figured God would just be with me to help keep me out of trouble as I stumbled through life. *Now I feel there is something certain in my future that He has planned for me. It is as if He is preparing me in these journeys of faith involving my children for something even bigger.*

More Lessons
October 16

I'm trying desperately to get to a peaceful place before the echocardiogram. I've picked up the Bible a couple of times, but I've only recently been reading it, so I'm not familiar with the verses that might bring me comfort. I've continued to read spiritual books and spend a lot of time listening to worship music. In fact, it is the music that helps me to focus the most.

The appointment is just a few days off, and there is so much anticipation and anxiety that I find myself in my bedroom with the music a lot. With so much time spent on a possible miracle, I have spent very little time on the alternative. *My son may die.*

But I can't think of my son dying. Every bit of me wants my baby to live, and I've prayed all week that a sign be revealed in this echocardiogram. *If a miracle of healing is truly God's plan for Steven, I need to see something that baffles the doctors.* Without this sign, I have told God and myself that I will prepare to part with our child.

Have We Misunderstood His Message?
October 18

"I'm sorry," he said as he was performing the echocardiogram. "There has been no change in your child's heart condition. The diagnosis is still Severe Hypoplastic Left Heart." He alluded to other complications, but I didn't ask for details. Tony squeezed my hand, but neither of us said anything. The doctor didn't understand our hopes for a miracle, so I'm sure he thought he was delivering news that I was already aware of. I held back the tears as he spoke.

"There is no need to come back for another echocardiogram; nothing will change," the doctor said as he finished putting the equipment away. "You should make final preparations for after delivery."

Tony and I didn't talk much on the way home from the hospital. As we approached the house, he said, "I need to go to the office, so I'm going to drop you off at the house and head in for a couple of hours." It was an excuse for him to be alone, but that was okay because I needed some alone time too.

Once in the house, I walked around, picked up a few toys, and then sat motionless at the dining room table for a very long time. Depression was setting in. Time passed, I don't know how much, but the phone rang and pulled me out of my daze. It was my mom, telling me she would bring the kids up to my house. She had been watching them for me, but I knew it would be good to get them home. It is easier to fight off depression when they are keeping me busy.

My heart aches so much right now. I have been trying to accept that God may take Steven, but from the volume of tears I have cried today, I'm not succeeding. It is as if a light inside of me has burned out.

Kim and I spoke briefly. "Nothing baffled the doctors," I said, with very little emotion in my voice.

> It is as if a light inside of me has burned out.

Still believing God has great plans for Steven, she replied, "I know it is hard to hang on, but I still think there will be a miracle." Her voice was quiet and less confident than usual. *I think she has a few questions of her own for God.*

"I'm confused and very, very tired. I don't believe that God has communicated so much hope for nothing, but I am too tired right now to think clearly. I feel like sleeping for a week."

Before we hung up, Kim challenged me, "Sandy, you need to believe God is in total control, or not in control at all."

I was quick to respond, "I don't doubt He is in total control. What I doubt is our understanding of His message. I'll give you a call in a few days."

The time has come to let go.

Letting Go
October 20

This has been a difficult few days, but I'm feeling stronger with each day that passes. I've been keeping myself busy with work from my office and scrapbooking some of the twins' photos. I've also made a list of things I need to do to begin preparing for the fate that awaits us. *If I do not begin the grieving process and accept that God may take Steven, I won't have the strength to handle it all in December after the delivery.*

I need to find peace. For me, that means finding that neutral place where I can accept whatever God's fate is for Steven. It means preparing for the worst, and praying for the best. It means believing God will give me the strength and courage to handle whatever lies ahead of me.

I called Loma Linda Hospital, hoping to learn more about donating Steven's tissue and corneas. The woman was not very clear, but my understanding is that Steven may not live long enough to develop tissue that can be transplanted. His corneas may be all that are viable. *It is painful that Steven's life can't benefit and bring hope to more children and families.* After hanging up the phone with Loma Linda, I cried some more.

Before dinner, Tony and I spoke about funeral arrangements. It was an agonizing and emotional conversation for both of us.

"Neither of us want to talk about this, but we really should discuss funeral arrangements," I said as he was fixing dinner and I was feeding the babies.

A spoonful of strained peas were headed toward Nicolas' mouth when he decided he was done with peas, smacking my hand and sending the spoon and peas flying. I was tired, frustrated, but too sad to be angry. Alexa let out a belly laugh over the fact that Nicolas' peas were on my face and in her hair. Not too concerned about the peas on my face, I looked at them both with watery eyes and softly said, "I only wish you two could know your brother."

I didn't think Tony had heard me, but he was quick to answer. "They will definitely know Steven." He sounded determined, but I could see that a tear was streaming down his face. "Through pictures, your journal, and through us. We won't let his memory die."

For the first time ever, Tony started talking with me about his sister Frances, who was born a few years before him, but died only a few days after birth. "My parents never talked to me about my sister. It was as if she was never born. I don't even know where she is buried, what her full name was, or how many days she lived." I was surprised to hear him talk about his sister. The only time he had mentioned her before was when I discovered her death certificate while going through old paperwork after his mother passed away.

We were both silent for a minute, although Nicolas and Alexa's chatter never slowed. I walked over to Tony and put my arms around him. "Nicolas and Alexa will know their brother. We will celebrate his life whether he lives or dies – in person or in spirit."

After a warm embrace, I continued, "I will call Forest Lawn Mortuary for funeral information and the costs involved. I don't want other people making the decisions for me while I'm in the hospital after the delivery. I just hope I can have a normal delivery, rather than another C-section. My recovery was so slow after the twins' C-Section, I fear I won't remember Steven if he dies too quickly."

"That won't happen," he said as he pulled away to get us both a tissue.

Even as we discuss death and burying our son, there is something very unreal about it. The reality is that I don't really believe Steven will die. The logical side of me tells me to prepare now, but my spirit keeps getting in the way. I hate the darkness and confusion I feel at this moment.

Have you ever found it difficult
to believe His promise and
trust His plan?

Chapter 8

They Think We're Crazy

"*Courage does not always roar. Sometimes it is a quiet voice at the end of the day, saying, 'I will try again tomorrow.'*"

~ *Mary Anne Radmacher* ~

Day-to-Day Stresses
October 25

It has been a difficult couple of days as lack of control has left me exhausted and frustrated. Poor Tony has been an easy target, so forgiving and patient.

He has been phasing out of his mortgage business, and making the transition to the insurance field. Passing both of his insurance tests, he is now licensed to sell most insurance products.

Even though he is learning the business quickly, it is not quite fast enough for either of us. It is hard for him with his time divided between two careers. He has his own way of doing things and, quite frankly, it drives me a little crazy. Working at the office with him has been so challenging.

Having this much stress at home and the office at the same time is not something I'm used to. In fact, I snapped while I was in the office on Thursday. And of all things, I flipped out over a toilet plunger. Tony had trouble getting past the toilet-plunger incident, taking awhile to realize the eruption had very little to do with plungers and everything to do with the chaos in my life. *Tension is building inside of me as we get closer to the delivery date. I'm having more difficulty focusing on my blessings and minimizing the strife in my life.*

Tony is under a lot of pressure of his own, and I hate to bring on more. When I try to explain my frustrations, he feels he must fix the problem. When I tell him I'm unhappy with the loss of control in my business since I have been consumed with this pregnancy, he thinks I'm blaming him for not doing more. When I tell him I'm stressed about money, he gets upset that he is not making more. When I tell him I want to plan for Steven in our lives, he feels bad that there is nothing he can do.

I love him for trying to make my life better, but sometimes I wish he would just listen to me ramble without trying to fix the things that can't always be fixed. I think most men have a need to fix. Listening without doing confounds them. Bless them all.

Final Preparations
November 7

A few minor contractions reminded me how quickly time is moving. With only four weeks to go, I have about a hundred things to accomplish before the delivery. I believe this is a nesting instinct that pregnant women experience as the birth approaches. I started a list so I wouldn't forget everything I need to do. Getting my life in order at this point has left me little time for my reading and writing.

Last week, Tony and I went to look at vans that can hold three car seats, and ended up buying one. It is a good choice for us, with or without Steven, and for a van, it is very nice. *I never thought I'd say that!* Socially, I am minivan adverse, even knowing it will make our lives easier. Because of dealer incentives, we ended up buying a new one, rather than a used one. *I love the smell of new cars. I also love the idea*

> *I held up remarkably well until they showed us the tiny caskets.*

that I have done something to plan for Steven. My precious Steven. I want so much for him to come home with us that I'm losing myself to "want" rather than staying neutral.

Yesterday, Mom and I went to the mall with the twins. She bought Steven his first outfit. It was baby blue velour with white trim. We did not discuss whether this would be the outfit we take Steven home from the hospital in or the outfit he is buried in, but I know the thought was on both of our minds. A tear was rolling down her cheek as she was paying for it.

Later that afternoon, we went by the mortuary to get information on funerals. I held up remarkably well until they showed us the tiny caskets. I fell apart.

I'm not sure if I was crying for Steven or for all of the parents who have purchased a casket for a baby. It was impossibly painful. We then drove to the area where the babies are buried. There was a woman in her twenties with her mother next to a gravesite; the young woman's baby was stillborn a week ago. My heart ached for her.

I've really slowed down these past few weeks. Exhausted when we left the mall, I started having cramps and back spasms by the time I got home. I'm not sure if they were contractions or not, but it reminded me again how close we are. I was only a week further along in my last pregnancy when I delivered the twins.

My feelings are mixed about this pregnancy ending. I've only gained 17 pounds, but I feel huge and uncomfortable. *I'm tired of being so tired.* As much as I would love to have this pregnancy over, I'm afraid of it ending. Steven is very much alive inside of me right now. His kicks are strong and constant. It's hard to believe he is so sick. Sometimes I wish it were January of next year, and other times, I wish time would stand still. *I'm not ready to give Steven up. I don't think I will ever be ready for that.*

Telling Doctors
November 13

Kim called this morning. Still feeling confident of the miracle to come, she has made plans to come to California for the delivery.

"My plane reservation is made. I'll be there on December 14th."

"That's fine, but I'm hoping Steven will be born on December 7th, since that was the day Tony and I first met and the day the embryos which turned out to be Nicolas and Alexa were implanted in me."

She sounded doubtful, "I don't think so. I had a vision that I met Steven in the hospital, and since I'm not scheduled to arrive in California until the fourteenth, I think his delivery will be closer to my arrival date."

I still don't know how to respond to her prophecies. I want to believe her interpretations are accurate, but I'm still skeptical. "We will know soon enough," I said. I wasn't giving up on the idea that Steven would be born on December 7th.

This afternoon, I had another doctor appointment. Tony went with me to ask more questions about the delivery, and to tell Dr. Rodrigues of our hopes for a miracle. He needed to understand our faith when we asked for another echocardiogram. We gave him a brief synopsis of what had transpired, and why we were not convinced Steven would die.

"I don't know if the hospital will perform another echocardiogram. Standard procedure would be to do no further evaluation because Hypoplastic Left Heart is not something that will heal or improve as the pregnancy progresses." After a long pause, he added, "I'm not sure we can request an echocardiogram based on faith. You need to talk to the neonatologist at the hospital."

Tony even helped me explain to Dr. Rodrigues our hopes for a miracle. Sensing the doctor's skepticism, Tony said, "We are not delusional in hoping for this miracle. Several people have communicated hope and healing involving Steven's situation, and we can't ignore all that has happened." Tony sounded confident, although the awkward silence when he finished was uncomfortable for me.

I don't think Dr. Rodrigues knew what to say after Tony's comments. He did not show much of a reaction, but I suppose doctors are trained not to. *I can't blame him for thinking we are crazy. Hearing the short version of why we think Steven might live had me thinking we were delusional!*

Dr. Rodrigues changed the subject, "On another note, the baby is head down so we are optimistic for the vaginal delivery you want."

With a very serious look on his face, he cautioned us. "But, I need you to know there is some risk to a vaginal delivery after having had the C-section. There is a small chance that your uterus could burst. Odds are less than 5 percent chance of this happening, but if it did, it would be extremely serious to your health."

Thinking for only a moment about the risk, "I will take the risk with the vaginal delivery so I will be alert during and after Steven's delivery. I can't take the chance of being heavily drugged after a C-section and miss Steven's brief life should he die."

Dr. Rodrigues nodded, "Do you want an emergency C-section if the baby's heart slows down while attempting the vaginal delivery?"

Again, with no hesitation, "If we did not have hope for Steven to be healed, I would not opt for the emergency procedure. But because we believe a miracle is a possibility, I would definitely want the emergency C-Section if it is necessary to keep Steven alive."

After we left, I felt relieved that we finally told Dr. Rodrigues about our hopes; in the past, I have always chickened out. I'm sure he thinks we're nuts, but I actually felt good, rather than depressed, when we left his office.

> *I can't blame him for thinking we are crazy. Hearing the short version of why we think Steven might live had me thinking we were delusional!*

I suppose a lot of people think we're nuts, and I guess I just don't care anymore.

Staying Focused
November 15

I was sitting on the couch in the living room writing when I heard Alexa wake up from her nap. She was calling, "Mama mama mama," and I decided to quickly go get her so she wouldn't wake up Nicolas.

"Mama's coming," I called out to her from where I was sitting. As I stood up, pain gripped my abdomen. I grabbed my side and doubled over, waiting for it to pass. I continued to talk to Alexa so she would know I was coming, but I knew her patience would dwindle quickly. I tried standing again, and for a second time, the sharp pain in my side stopped me in my tracks. I debated crawling up the stairs, but knew I wouldn't be able to lift her out of the crib.

I picked up the phone that was on the coffee table near me. "How soon can you come to the house?" I don't like to cry when I talk to my mom, but she could hear me fighting back tears.

"I can be there in a few minutes. Are you feeling okay?"

"Not really. I can't walk again today. The pain is so bad …" I didn't finish the sentence. "Alexa just woke from her nap and is starting to cry, and I can't get upstairs to get her out of her crib."

"Don't worry. I'll be right there."

For ten days, I have fought the pain, and I'm about at the end of my rope. The first day I started having trouble, I tried to ignore the situation. But the pain near the scar tissue from my C-section intensified to the point that I could barely walk yesterday, and I couldn't walk at all today.

The kids have been great lately, even with the challenges I've had in caring for them. They must understand that something is not quite right with Mommy these days. They have been a little more patient than usual as they watch me struggle to fix their lunch or dress them. Nicolas has been into shadow boxing lately, and Alexa walks around yelling "Mom!" She rarely says "Mommy" or "Mama," just "Mom" and then waits for my reaction. Her other favorite new phrase is "poo-poo butt." She doesn't even have a load in her diaper when she says it.

I bought their Christmas outfits with all the accessories. Alexa has been wearing her new black patent leather shoes and pink tights to break them in and cries when I take them off of her. She still likes to wear things on her head and wants me to leave her shirts dangling off her head when I change her at night. *She looks like a little nun.* She has also been into books lately and loves to sit on everyone's lap and look at the pictures. Nicolas doesn't have a lot of patience for books and would rather just tear out the pages.

Steven has been really active these days. It is becoming more uncomfortable when he moves around and kicks. It's great to feel him move, but the level of his activity surprises me. During my first pregnancy, the twins were too crowded to move much.

Nicolas saw ripples moving across my belly today and came and laid his head on my stomach. It was a photo moment, but no one was around to take a picture. Alexa then came over and put her hands on my stomach, and I hugged them both against Steven. "We are having a group hug," I whispered as they smiled their clueless smiles. "I hope we can always have group hugs that include Steven."

Concerns
November 17

Nicolas and Alexa had their fifteen-month-old checkup and shots for mumps, measles, and rubella yesterday. While we were at the pediatrician's office, I told their doctor about Steven's heart condition. "We are confused and very apprehensive about what is going to happen after the delivery. After my conversation with Dr. Rodrigues last week, I'm concerned that we may have problems getting an echocardiogram performed after the delivery. In the minds of doctors, Steven's diagnosis is not going to change so there is no need for more tests." I explained briefly why I thought God might work a miracle through Steven.

"I've seen a few miracles in my day," she said as she lifted Nicolas off the examination table where he was starting to squirm. *Thank you for not questioning my faith.*

"I'm upset because if we don't have another echocardiogram performed after his birth, we are not going to know if Steven has been healed or if he might be dying in our arms within hours to days after his birth. I'll be emotional enough after this long and difficult pregnancy and delivery, and I will need to prepare to rejoice or let go."

The pediatrician continued to listen to my concerns. "I don't fault the doctors for making decisions based on medical facts and not faith, but there is no peace in it for us. How long will they make us wait before further evaluation? A day? A week? Two weeks? I'll have a mental breakdown by then."

As I spoke, she continued to take notes. "I don't think it will be a problem to have Steven's heart evaluated again after birth." She handed me a piece of paper with a fax number on it. "Fax over the medical records so I can talk to the neonatologist at the hospital."

Within an hour after I faxed the information, she had arranged a consultation for us.

A Rainbow
November 19

This morning we left Nicolas and Alexa with Grace, her husband, and her kids. As usual, the twins were thrilled to be visiting some of their favorite people and never looked back as Tony and I left for church. I was feeling a little depressed and hoped something in the sermon might lift my spirits. Consumed with thoughts of Steven, I had trouble focusing on the readings and sermon. He was kicking a lot and Tony reached over and laid his hand on my stomach as he has done so many times before.

Feeling scared and anxious, I started thinking how little time we have left to enjoy this time with Steven. In fact, we will only be in church two or three more times before Steven is born. Tears came to my eyes and I tried to focus on something more positive. Looking up, I saw a rainbow and an image of Christ in the stained glass window. In all of the times I have been in this church, I never noticed the rainbow before.

Doleen and I spoke after church for a few minutes. She is still praying for us all. We also spoke with the pastor and briefly explained the situation. Assuring us God has a plan for Steven, he told us to try and find peace with God's will. He blessed me with the Sacrament of the Sick and prayed for Steven.

He answered a question of mine by telling me that a Catholic Church service is not done before the burial of an infant. I was unaware that the main purpose of the church service is to ask for forgiveness of sin for the deceased. Since an infant is without sin, there is no need for a Mass.

I wonder why the Church can't do a service just for closure to the family. Note to self: Talk to Uncle Jack about performing a service for us... if a service is necessary.

The Hospital Consultation
November 22

This morning we met with the neonatologist who relieved my biggest concern when he agreed to perform another echocardiogram after Steven's birth. He even told me there is a special room we can stay in if I am discharged before Steven dies.

I held up remarkably well throughout the consultation...until we discussed organ donation. "My understanding based on conversations with previous doctors is that Steven's organ donation will be limited to corneas and possibly tissue." I looked toward the doctor who had done most of the talking for confirmation, but he didn't answer immediately. "Is that right?"

"Unfortunately, you were given incorrect information," he said. "A newborn's corneas and tissue are too fragile for successful transplant. Your son will have nothing to offer in the way of organ donation."

There was an awkward silence as I fought off tears. *My hope of helping other families as a way of bringing purpose to Steven's life is gone. I have so much love for Steven already, and I will never regret having carried him to term. But the feelings of loss will be far greater than if I had ended the pregnancy in August.*

Tony asked a few more questions, but I had drifted off into my own thoughts and didn't pay attention to the rest of their discussion.

I'm Not Ready!
November 27

Last night, I started having contractions at regular intervals. Panic seized me, as the end is so inevitably close. I am mentally unprepared to go into labor. I have not found peace. If I could only find peace in his living or dying, I would be prepared for anything. *But how do I find peace in Steven dying? Is it even possible?*

Tony and I talked a little about my restless feelings today. I couldn't help but ask, "What odds would you place on a miracle that Steven's heart will be healed?" Knowing Tony would not make odds, I asked the question anyway. *I'm desperate for hope.*

"I don't want to go down that road with you right now, but what I do believe is that Steven will be healed. I'm just not sure it will be a physical healing of his heart."

This was too vague for me so I pressed on. "So that means you think he will die?"

Tony sighed and hesitated. I knew he didn't want to answer, "I believe God will make us all okay with whatever the outcome is. I'm happy to have had Steven in our lives for even this short time, and I'm ready to give him up if it is God's will. I will be sad, but we need to focus on all of the people Steven has touched, and how much closer to God our entire family has grown." He looked at me with concern. "Promise me you won't lose faith if he dies."

His words made sense, but I was still irritated. "I will not lose faith in God if Steven dies, but I will definitely question the ride we have been on. So much has revolved around the belief that Steven might be healed that I will question what part of the growth with God was real and what part was based on misinterpretation of His word. I will not be angry or believe that God did not fulfill His promise to us if Steven dies. Instead, I will believe it was never His intention to heal his broken heart."

Not sure whether I was making any sense, I went on, "If we had never received any words or impressions that Steven might be healed, I would have grown with God, knowing Steven would die shortly after birth. I would have leaned on God through this difficult time, knowing that eventually He would bring me peace with the death of our son. But that is not what happened, as I was given incredible hope."

Pausing, I tried to clarify my thoughts for both of us. "Steven will die, and I won't understand the promise of hope and healing that God has communicated to so many people."

"God, bring her peace."

I walked over to the bay window and stared outside. Neither of us spoke for several minutes and when I did, it was barely audible. "Would God find hope and promise in the death of a child? And even if He does, would He expect me to find hope and promise in my child dying?"

Tony walked over and put his arms around me just to silence me. I heard him whisper under his breath, "God, bring her peace."

Have you ever been so overwhelmed
that you could see no light — only
darkness with a fading rainbow
on the horizon?

Chapter 9

The Countdown

"Come to me, all you who are weary and burdened, and I will give you rest."

~ Matthew 11:28 NIV ~

More Frustrations
December 1

This has been one heck of a challenging week. I am feeling a little more at peace with Steven's situation, but I have felt less peace regarding the rest of my life. I am as mentally prepared as I'm going to be for Steven's delivery, but I'm physically drained.

Nicolas has had a lingering fever, but is getting better. Alexa came down with a 104° fever on Saturday. We monitored her fever all night, and to no surprise, Nicolas' fever came back on Sunday along with terrible congestion. Breathing treatments began for both of them on Monday, which is a challenge in itself. Trying to keep two fifteen-month-old babies still for a fifteen-minute treatment is a real trick.

By Tuesday, Nicolas' congestion was so bad that our doctor sent us to the hospital for chest x-rays. She told me if there were any signs of pneumonia, she would be admitting him to the hospital. Barely able to stand or walk myself, I was spinning out of control at the thought of spending all day and night with him hooked up to an IV. Memories of Alexa's one-week stay in the hospital with RSV in January are still too vivid in my mind.

Due to my advanced stage of pregnancy, I could not hold Nicolas while they did the x-rays. Feeling helpless, I sat with Alexa in the waiting room. My mom went in with him, but I could hear him screaming down the hallway. *I can't even take care of my own kids when they need me most. God, how much more can I handle?* Nearly in tears from exhaustion, I became scared when cramping and contractions started.

We finally left the hospital, and a couple of hours later, the pediatrician called to tell me Nicolas' chest was clear, but we should continue medications and breathing treatments every four hours. *What a relief!* Tony was in a meeting all day, so my cousin came over to watch the babies so I could run to the office to wrap up a few details. Well, maybe not run. It was more of a slow waddle, as I was still having contractions. I was exhausted, but on a mission. My adrenalin had kicked in, and I was determined to get through everything while I still had the chance.

By the time I got home from the office, I was having contractions every 20-30 minutes. By 10:00 p.m., they were about ten minutes apart. Part of me wanted to go into full labor, but most of me did not. I was worried about Nicolas and wanted him healthy before Tony and I head to the hospital. Finally, I climbed into bed around 11:00 p.m. and set my alarm for every couple of hours to check on the kids' fevers throughout the night.

I was up and down all night checking the kids' temperatures, and by Wednesday morning, I was beyond tired. I should have rested, but Nicolas was looking better, so I decided to keep my appointment to have the kids' Christmas pictures taken. *We have to act as normal as possible for holidays, no matter how abnormal life is right now or how unbelievably exhausted I am.*

I may have let my determination rest if I had known what awaited us.

We have to act as normal as possible for holidays, no matter how abnormal life is right now or how unbelievably exhausted I am.

It had been a long morning getting ready, and the pain in my side was back. My mom suggested I use the wheelchair since the mall would be crowded and I could barely walk. She pushed me with both kids on my lap, which helped with my fatigue, but my hopes of a quick trip didn't come to fruition. When we got into the photo studio, complete chaos ensued. It ended up being an hour-long wait, even with an appointment. I really wanted the photos or we would have left. Mom chased the kids around while I sat there and felt bad for not being more helpful.

By the time they called us in, the kids were tired and cranky and I think Nicolas associated the photo set table with the table he sat on for his x-ray at the hospital yesterday. Needless to say, he was not happy. When we sat him on the table...or at least we tried... he immediately screamed and cried as he scrambled to get away. Of course, Alexa started yelling and would not sit still either. I just wanted to scream. Or cry. Or both. *Why is everything so difficult these days?*

I called Tony on the way home, trying to avoid sounding as desperate as I was beginning to feel. "Can you get home early today?"

"I can probably wrap things up soon. Is everything okay?"

"Yeah, we're okay, but it has been another rough day. Pictures were a bust, I'm exhausted, and Mom needs a break from all of us." I looked over at my mother, who was driving my van. She smiled at my comment, but couldn't deny there was some truth to it.

"I can be home in an hour. Is there anything I can bring you or do for you before I get there?"

"All I really need is a long nap," I paused to think if there was anything else I wanted. "Oh and if you really want to make me happy, maybe you can put the Christmas tree up early. I need something to lift my spirits."

By the time I finished my nap that afternoon, the tree was up. I was feeling good enough to help Tony decorate it, which improved my mood tremendously.

I really enjoy the holidays and Tony gets into them too. Every year, he sets up a huge lighted city around the tree, and last year he added trains that chugged through the city. The kids love it. We also buy a new family ornament each year. This year's has Steven's name on it along with all of ours. *I love seeing his name in print.*

We hung the family ornament in front where I could easily see it, but high enough for the babies not to be able to pull it off.

We have five stockings this year. I found a small white stocking made of satin with white fur lining. I glued some baby-blue piping on it, spelling Steven's name.

"Do you want to come in here while I hang Steven's stocking?" I called to Tony who was working on the trains in the living room. Our fireplace is in the family room, so every year, we hang the stockings on the fireplace mantle, and set up the large artificial tree with the trains around it in front of the bay window in the living room. We also buy a small live tree for the family room because I love the smell of Christmas trees.

"Yeah, just give me a minute. I'm almost done here." After a couple seconds, I heard, "No Nicolas. Don't do that."

I set Steven's stocking on the side table while I opened the box with the small bear stocking holder. The stocking holder is only a couple inches tall, but it has a child-like look to it and is perfect for Steven's small white satin stocking. Alexa walked over to his stocking, picked it up, and touched the baby-blue piping that spelled STEVEN.

"That is your little brother's stocking," I said as she put the soft satin stocking up to her cheek. She loves silky things, and I smiled as she rubbed her face on his stocking, but I feared there would be remnants of lunch left behind on the white satin, "Can Mama have the stocking?" I held out my hand and Alexa walked over to me and relinquished the stocking.

"Can you call Nicolas in there? He is really slowing me down." I could hear the frustration in Tony's voice, but he calmly and quietly finished with "Nicolas, give that back to Daddy and go see your Mama."

"Hey, Nicolas. Buddy, can you come help Mama?" I set Steven's stocking back down on the side table so I could finish getting all of our stocking holders out of their boxes and up on the mantle.

I heard Nicolas running through the kitchen in my direction and glanced over my shoulder to see him stop in front of Steven's stocking, pick it up, and start pulling the piping off it.

"Nicolas! No!" He looked up at me and smiled with no plans of stopping, but it gave me just enough time to rescue the stocking.

Just then Tony came walking in the family room and scooped Nicolas up in his arms. "You little troublemaker." He kissed him on his head and walked over to me.

"Come help us hang Steven's stocking," I said to Alexa, and although she had no idea what I said, she walked in our direction. I put my arms out for Nicolas since he is lighter and easier for me to hold, and Tony picked up Alexa.

> That is your little brother's stocking."

I picked up Steven's stocking and put it on his stocking holder while flattening a piece of the piping that was lifted from Nicolas pulling on it. It was a sweet moment, and neither Tony nor I said anything for a few seconds.

"What do you think, Buddy?" I looked at Nicolas who was fascinated for the moment with Steven's stocking and bear holder that hung next to the other still empty holders. "I bet you're wondering where yours is, aren't you?" I reached into the box on the chair next to the fireplace and handed him his stocking. I helped him hold it with his little fingers and put it on his stocking holder. Alexa was watching and lunged in my direction when I held hers up. She knew exactly what to do with it so, with only a little assistance from Daddy, she put her own stocking up too.

"It's strange that I do not feel Steven will die, and yet I have not allowed myself to focus for any length of time on him coming home." Tony was still holding Alexa and walked over and put his arm around me. A tear slid down my face, and I put Nicolas down and wiped the tear away. "No nursery is set up." I paused, "It's like being in a twilight zone. I can't imagine life with or without Steven." My voice barely a whisper, Tony said nothing but gave my shoulder a squeeze.

I couldn't take my eyes off the stockings. "There have been only two scenarios that play over and over in my mind that involve Steven coming home. The first is a big sign on the garage door that says 'Welcome Home, Steven!' when we drive home from the hospital. The second is the five of us going to church on Christmas Eve." I reached out and rubbed Steven's name on his stocking before walking away to see where Nicolas had gone.

How Strong Am I?
December 2

Last night as I was working on this manuscript, I heard Nicolas crying in bed. It was about 10:30 p.m. and I was so tired and relaxed that I didn't want to move.

"Can you check on Nicolas?" I yelled to Tony from the couch. My body felt like it was weighted down with a ton of bricks. I was wrapped up in my favorite blanket, feet elevated, drinking hot chocolate while typing.

He didn't answer, but I could hear him walking up the stairs in the direction of the baby room.

"Oh my God!" he yelled from the babies' room a few seconds later.

Fear gripped me as I jumped to my feet, forgetting about the physical pain that usually comes when I move too quickly. I was to the steps when Tony came running down the stairs with Nicolas, whose crying had escalated to screaming. Tony looked panicked

He does not look like my baby.

and was holding Nicolas with one arm, while the other hand slid down the railing, holding him steady. He stopped at the base of the stairs so I could take a better look at Nicolas.

Stunned at what I saw, the entire right side of his face, jaw, and ear was so swollen that the shape of his head looked distorted. *He does not look like my baby.* Tears filled my tired eyes, but I remained calm.

"Put him in his car seat while I call Mom to come up and stay with Alexa," I said to Tony.

Within ten minutes, we were off to the hospital, and five hours later, doctors told us that Nicolas has the mumps. *Just what we don't need.* Apparently, the virus he had been sick with made him more susceptible to getting mumps from the vaccination he received two weeks earlier. The doctor told us the other side of his face may also swell, and the fever will probably be back in the next couple of days.

He was still congested and miserable from the other virus, and now this. And the doctors warned us that he would most likely get a lot worse before getting better, which takes a good 7-10 days. Alexa is also susceptible. *So I'm waiting for yet another shoe to drop.*

We got home from the hospital at 4:00 a.m. and I dropped into bed as soon as my mother walked out the door. Not surprisingly, Alexa woke up at 6:00 a.m. feeling rested and ready for the day. There was no time for a nap today, so I'm deliriously tired.

I wish I could sleep until January.

Details
December 8

Another week has gone by. I thought yesterday would be the delivery day, but next week is looking more probable. Kim is flying out on the fourteenth, so we are hoping Steven will be born on the thirteenth or fourteenth. We are blessed with a great deal of support, but it is going to be a very chaotic time. So many friends and family are affected by what is happening. So many prayers for one little baby.

Getting Nicolas and Alexa healthy before leaving them to deliver Steven is my number one priority. Never having been apart from them overnight, I get anxious just thinking about it. With all that will be happening with Steven's arrival, I don't want to worry about them. Grace said she will take care of them, so I know I shouldn't worry.

Alexa is still fighting the virus, but has no sign of mumps. They are still getting breathing treatments for their chest congestion, and I pray they will be better soon. Tony hasn't been feeling well either and casually mentioned he didn't think he has had the mumps or the shots to prevent them. *I should probably be worried about him, but I'm so overloaded that I'm leaving that one to God.*

Nicolas had been doing much better a few days ago, but his temperature soared again last night, and we noticed some swelling on the other side of his face. It's still mumps related, but I feel fortunate it was not a severe case. *Oh Lord, please don't let me get sick right now.*

I was amused, in a twisted sort of way, over the conversation I had with the on-call pediatrician last weekend. He thought it was very unusual that Nicolas was diagnosed with mumps at the hospital the night before; he told me the odds were so low of that happening that he could hardly believe it was mumps. *Welcome to my life!*

> *Odds mean nothing to me anymore. Thinking back over the past couple of years, nothing involving odds makes any sense in my life.*

Odds mean nothing to me anymore. Thinking back over the past couple of years, nothing involving odds makes any sense in my life. I was told the odds of having premature ovarian failure were less than 1%. The odds of having IVF success with twins were less than 3%. I was told the odds of getting pregnant with my own eggs were less than half a percent without medical intervention, and yet I am pregnant with Steven.

The odds of gestational diabetes are 5-10% for general pregnancies and less for someone like me with no history of contributing factors. The odds of a baby with a congenital heart defect are 2-3%, and less than a fraction of a percent for a Severe Hypoplastic Left Heart like my son has. *So much for "the odds."*

Now just to keep it exciting, there are a couple of odds with yet-to-be-determined results. I have a 5% chance of my uterus bursting if we do a vaginal delivery, and the odds of Steven living are 0%. The latter is such a sobering statistic, and yet my belief in God continues to bring me hope. The God factor makes odds irrelevant.

Still overdoing everything, I really need to slow down and reflect on this journey and the direction in which my life is going. I'm not a patient person, and I want every detail taken care of before going to the hospital, which is obviously impossible.

Paying bills, organizing files, finishing office paperwork, taking care of sick babies, and doing Christmas shopping were on the agenda this past week. This was the first time I even had a chance to sit down and write. Physically, I'm uncomfortable, but I'm in fairly good spirits.

At my weekly doctor appointment yesterday, I met with the third doctor in the medical group. He was already familiar with my situation and my hopes for a miracle for Steven.

"So did Dr. Rodrigues fill you in on our situation, or is my file flagged with 'nut alert?'"

"Dr. Rodrigues filled me in, and no, your file is not red flagged with a 'nut alert.'" He sounded amused as he answered, but I didn't believe him.

"So is she ready to have labor induced?" Tony asked, sounding hopeful. The holidays are so close that Tony wants me to deliver as soon as possible.

"Unfortunately, you're still not ready for us to induce labor," he said. "Let's have you come back Monday to see if we can possibly induce on Wednesday the thirteenth."

I looked in Tony's direction and said, "It will be good timing with Kim coming in on the fourteenth." I was amused with the timing of Kim's arrival and thought back to her vision of meeting Steven for the first time in the hospital.

Countdown to Delivery
December 13

This past Monday I went for my appointment with Dr. Rodrigues, and he decided to induce labor tonight around midnight. It was a busy couple of days, but I was able to get almost everything done. Yesterday, I didn't schedule anything in hopes of a quiet, peaceful day to collect my thoughts and prepare for the outcome with Steven. As usual, things were crazy. In the morning, someone wanted to buy my T-Bird that the van replaced so Tony was out cleaning and waxing the car so we could meet the buyer later in the afternoon.

As we were racing around getting ready to meet him, the priest from our church asked if he could stop by. He wasn't able to make it in the afternoon as we had originally planned, so he told me he was coming over in fifteen minutes.

"Stop waxing the car and get in here," I yelled out the front door.

Because of the urgency in my voice, Tony dropped everything and came running in the door. "Are you okay?" he asked when he saw me racing through the living room.

"Quick! Help me clean this house," I shrieked as I shoved some boxes in the coat closet. Tony wasn't moving, just staring at me as if I had lost my mind. "Father Ned is on his way over now, and I don't want him seeing this house looking like this! Don't just stand there. Move!"

Tony had boxes everywhere from having just put up the trains and lighted city around the Christmas tree. My carpet was barely visible. He began racing boxes to the garage, and I threw everything else in the family room and said a little prayer that Father Ned would not venture past the living room.

We had the living room looking presentable when Tony looked at me and said, "The house is looking pretty good, but have *you* looked in the mirror lately?" My hair was a mess, I was wearing no makeup, and had not had a chance to shower.

I laughed at his comment. "No time to fix myself up; I figure Father Ned will see me on better days, but chances are he will never be in our house again." I shrugged my shoulders, "Twisted priorities?"

Tony chuckled, "Well at least go brush your teeth and hair. You don't want to scare him off before he says his blessing."

Father Ned said several prayers, including a "Blessing for Mothers." Not long after he arrived, my mother walked through the front door. I had called her a few minutes before, asking if she could come up while Father Ned prayed for us. She quietly sat down on the couch next to me, as Father Ned had already started his prayer.

It was quiet for only a few seconds after her arrival. Within seconds of her sitting on the couch, "Nananana" could be heard from the gated community where the kids were playing. They could see the back of my mom's head and were determined to let her know they were waiting for her. My mom smiled at me but did not acknowledge the kids, hoping they would quiet down. The chanting got louder. Both of them were leaning against the gate and calling for her. I'm sure they were confused that *their* nana would be in the house and not come and see them, as was the routine.

It was a huge distraction, but Father Ned continued his prayers as if he didn't hear all of the commotion. I nudged my mom and pointed for her to move to the other side of the couch so they wouldn't see her, and after another minute or so, they settled down.

The prayers were comforting, and for a brief moment in time, I felt peace. When he finished, Father Ned mentioned he would be out of town and might miss the delivery. He told us that if we want to baptize Steven, we could do it ourselves if he isn't able to be there. Tony and my mom listened to his brief instructions on baptizing while I walked over to Nicolas and Alexa who started the chattering all over again when they saw their nana stand up.

Father Ned walked over to Nicolas and Alexa and said a quick blessing over them. We thanked him for coming, and within minutes, our chaotic day continued.

We raced off to sell the T-Bird, and later spent the afternoon cleaning the rest of the house and packing for the kids. I was able to spend a little quiet time with Steven, but not as much as I had hoped for.

I slipped into the twins' bedroom while they were napping just to spend some quiet time with my three children. I moved the rocking chair between their cribs and watched them sleep. They looked so peaceful, and I rocked Steven while watching them. Steven was awake most of the time, and I felt his kicks as I rubbed my stomach. Tony came looking for me and found me humming "Amazing Grace" while watching the babies sleep.

"I've been looking for you," he whispered as he quietly walked in the room.

"I'm just getting my last dose of babies before we drop them off with Grace," I smiled up at him. "I know I will be preoccupied, but it is still going to be hard to be away from these two. I've never been away from them for more than a few hours."

"They will be just fine," he assured me with a gentle touch on my arm.

"I know they will be fine; it's their mama that I'm worried about," I whispered, referring to myself in third person. Just then, Steven kicked a couple of times.

"Not all of your kids are napping," I said as I took Tony's hand and placed it on my belly. Tony knelt down beside me with his hand on

I am tired and stressed and figure it will be a long night for me, but one of us needs to be rested for tomorrow.

my stomach, waiting for kicks while watching Nicolas and Alexa sleep. After a few minutes he left, but I continued rocking for about twenty more minutes before leaving their room to finish packing.

About 5:00 p.m., we dropped Nicolas and Alexa off at Grace's house and went to dinner and a movie before heading to the hospital. The movie helped to pass the time, although my thoughts remained on what would unfold over the next few days. Tony and I were both quiet at dinner; neither of us had much to say.

Tony checked me into the hospital and went home just after 11 p.m. to get some sleep after I assured him. "I am tired and stressed and figure it will be a long night for me, but one of us needs to be rested for tomorrow."

It is now 6:00 a.m. on Wednesday the thirteenth. I'm sitting up in my hospital bed, writing what I hope will be the very happy ending to my book. I am so tired that I can hardly see straight, and yet I can't get my mind off of Steven long enough to sleep. I haven't slept a wink, and with my labor pains intensifying and my blood pressure being checked every fifteen minutes, I have missed any chance at sleep. The nurse just moved me into a birthing room that is much bigger and brighter than the room I started in last night. It has lifted my spirits. *I'm scared and anxious so I'll write a little more. Writing helps me to channel my fear and feel hope.*

I'm praying that the drugs to induce labor are successful because both the nurse and doctor warned me they could bring me to full labor without my cervix dilating. Aside from losing Steven, my worst nightmare would be to have a C-section after full labor. *I don't want to be too drugged up and miss time with my Steven.*

The pain is coming on stronger and I'm getting crankier. I hurt and I'm very hungry.

I called Tony a few minutes ago and was surprised he was still at the house.

"I thought you would be here by now. What is taking you so long?" It was more of a demand than a question.

"Is there a reason I need to be there right now?" he replied, concerned that he had misunderstood the timeline.

I softened up a bit, "No, but I need you here with me now. I've been up all night. I'm feeling frayed and tired, and the pain is getting worse." I paused for a couple of seconds and added, "and I'm really hungry so be sure to eat before you get here. They won't allow me any food, and I don't want to watch you eat."

"I'll be there soon," he said. "And I know you are scared…we are both scared, but we will get through this." I didn't answer as I fought back tears. "Love you," he said before hanging up.

God, help me to deal with the pain, and bring me through this safely so I can go home to my beautiful family. I pray with all of my heart that Steven goes home with us. I'm not able to find a place of peace with the death of my son. But if You choose to take Steven, please give me the grace to part with him. And God, as I have prayed so many times before, give Tony and me the strength to get through this day.

Have there been times in your life
when you felt that you couldn't
handle one more thing, and the
challenges just kept coming?

Chapter 10

An Angel is Born

*"God danced the day
you were born!
You are loved.
You are beautiful.
You are a gift of God,
His own possession.
You are a gift to all the world,
His gift of love to us.
You are His."*

~ Richard Kramer ~

The Delivery

When I stopped writing, it was 6:30 a.m. on December 13th. The contractions intensified, and I was no longer able to concentrate on capturing my moment-by-moment feelings and thoughts about Steven's impending birth. The shooting pain down my hip and back was so uncomfortable that it was hard to focus on anything other than how miserable I felt.

I did not want the epidural too soon, so I tried using my Lamaze training, but I still was not mentally prepared for the pain. I was given an epidural around 1:00 p.m., and by 3:00 p.m., I had dilated to five centimeters. Dr. Rodrigues came by for a visit shortly afterwards. "Things are moving slowly, but I'm pleased with the progress and don't think a C-section will be necessary," he said, looking at a chart by my bed.

"That's good to hear. Do you have any idea how much longer?"

"You've still got a ways to go. Just to confirm, you want a C-section to prolong the baby's life, should there be complications during delivery?" Although his words and tone were very clinical, I think I saw sympathy on his face as he asked the question.

I nodded. "I'm still not convinced Steven will die, so I definitely want the surgery if complications arise." I glanced over at Tony who smiled, assuring me this was a good decision that we both agreed on.

About an hour later, Kim called for the third time. Even with the epidural, I was still in a lot of pain and not taking any calls except from my mother and Kim. I let out a little moan from the most recent contraction and said, "The doctor was here awhile ago and told me things are still looking optimistic for a normal delivery."

"Sandy, I still believe you will be going into surgery. I've had more than one vision of you in an operating room." Kim was convinced a surgery was imminent, but I wasn't.

"I hope you're wrong." Too tired and in too much pain to be pleasant on the phone, I ended the conversation quickly. "We probably won't talk again until after my delivery. Keep the prayers coming, and I'll talk to you later. I'll have Mom keep you updated on our recovery."

My mom had been with me earlier and then left with my dad to get some lunch. She said she would be back to relieve Tony so he could get a bite to eat. He was looking really worn out. After hanging up the phone, I got out of bed again and began rocking in the chair near the bed.

"What an incredibly slow process," I whined to Tony, who was flipping through a magazine.

"Yeah, not as time effective as the twins." He closed the magazine and looked up at me. "I think our appointment for the twins' surgery was at five, and by six o'clock, we had us a couple of babies."

> Not knowing what the problem was, I could feel the fear creeping in on me.

"I sure miss those babies right now. Can you bring me the photo album?" I pointed to the little album of photos that Grace had put together for me to bring to the hospital. Tony brought it to me and moved his chair near mine so we could flip through the photos of Nicolas and Alexa.

"We are blessed." I closed the album and stood up to stretch before another contraction came.

"Yes, we are," Tony replied, and then more softly, said it again, "Yes, we are."

The next couple of hours were long ones, but by 6:00 p.m., I was dilated to nearly seven centimeters. Thinking things were fine, I was surprised when two nurses came running into my room with a doctor a few steps behind. They looked concerned as they adjusted some of my equipment. Not knowing what the problem was, I could feel the fear creeping in on me.

"Okay, it has stabilized," the doctor said. He and the two nurses visibly relaxed. The two nurses stepped back from the equipment they had adjusted and watched the monitors. One of them looked up and gave me a little smile, possibly to reassure me.

I wasn't sure if it was my vital signs or Steven's that were not stable, but before I could ask, the nurse (who had never taken her eyes off the monitor) yelled something, and everyone started moving quickly again. The equipment they were all focused on was monitoring Steven, so I knew my baby was in trouble. Tony was standing out of the way, concentrating on the monitors, trying to make sense of what they were looking at. *What is happening? Are we losing him before we even see him?* Feeling so helpless, I closed my eyes while tears streamed down my face.

For the second time, they were able to stabilize Steven, but only for a few minutes. Tony had just sat down on the edge of my bed when several medical people came rushing into my room. I wasn't sure if they were doctors, nurses, or technicians. Hospital bed and all, I was being rushed out of my room and down the hallway to the operating room. As panic gripped me, I yelled, "Tony! Where are you? You're coming, right?" I didn't want him being left behind, and I couldn't see if he was following us. My chest was tight and I was finding it hard to breathe. My hands trembled as I tried to hold onto the bar on the edge of the bed.

> *What is happening? Are we losing him before we even see him? Feeling so helpless, I closed my eyes while tears streamed down my face.*

"Your baby is showing signs of stress, and your blood pressure is dropping." A doctor was trying to explain what was happening, as we raced with seven or eight people into an operating room. "We will be performing an emergency C-section in a few minutes." Although his voice was calm, he didn't look calm to me. *Where is Dr. Rodrigues? I want Dr. Rodrigues, not someone I don't know.*

I was terrified. Everything around me was spinning. So many people were rushing around the operating room. My body began trembling out of control, so much so that the nurse needed to strap my arms down. Although I was not making any sound, tears poured down my face. *Where is Tony?* I looked around and didn't see him.

"Where is my husband?" I asked the nurse who was strapping my arms down.

"Don't worry. You'll be fine."
He gently stroked my face and hair as I looked up at him.

"They will bring him into the operating room as soon as he is prepped." She moved quickly to the other side of the operating table.

I turned my head to the door just as he walked in. "Wait here until they have her ready for surgery," a nurse told Tony before she grabbed some supplies and headed back in my direction. A couple of seconds later, Dr. Rodrigues walked briskly into the room.

It comforted me to know both Tony and Dr. Rodrigues were there, but my body was still trembling uncontrollably. Staring at the ceiling, I closed my eyes and tried to block out the confusion that was happening around me. A moment later, I felt someone's hands on my face. I opened my eyes, expecting to see Tony, but instead saw the anesthesiologist who had given me an epidural earlier. Wearing an operating gown and mask, he leaned over the top of my head so he was only four or five inches above my face. "Don't worry. You'll be fine." He gently stroked my face and hair as I looked up at him.

His compassion was overwhelming, and as I stared into his eyes, I felt my body begin to relax. He stayed with me for a minute or so while the other doctors finished preparing for surgery. His words helped to calm me, and I felt some peace within the chaos. Out of the corner of my eye, I saw Tony watching, and then walking over to me just before the operation began.

"Please don't give me too much medication," I said to Dr. Rodrigues before he began the surgery. "I might miss out on Steven's short life." I was speaking so softly that I don't think he heard. If he did hear me, he didn't answer.

As they pulled Steven from me, I heard his little cry and got a quick glance at his perfect face before they whisked him away for the echocardiogram.

While in recovery, Dr. Rodrigues came over to me and began talking, but I was barely awake from the anesthesia. "The C-section turned out to be as critical for you as it was for Steven. The scarring from the first C-section was such that had you continued with the vaginal delivery, your uterus would have burst."

So tired and heavily medicated, I heard what he said but was unable to reply or even care about what he was saying. I was still having trouble keeping my eyes open, and he told me we would talk later. Tony was standing near me and Dr. Rodrigues continued talking with him while I fell back asleep.

The echocardiogram took about an hour, and I fought sleep while waiting in recovery. I barely remember the doctor coming in with the results.

Tony was next to me when the doctor started speaking. "Your son still has a severe case of Hypoplastic Left Heart." He talked a little more, but I didn't hear anything being said. I had heard enough. The results were not as we had hoped and prayed. Steven's diagnosis remained unchanged. *His heart is still broken. He will only live a day or two.*

Lying in the recovery bed with my eyes shut, I was limp and non-responsive. It may have been the heavy medication from the operation, or possibly God had prepared me for what they were going to tell us. I heard Tony ask, "Were there any changes to the severity of his condition so that reconstruction of his heart might be a viable option?"

"There are other issues besides the poor condition of his heart which would be impossible to successfully reconstruct with surgeries," the doctor replied. I was so out of it, I heard the doctor but had no reaction to his words. I knew it was bad. I drifted in and out while Tony asked more questions.

As I woke up in recovery, I remembered the conversation with the doctor and began to feel complete despair. I kept my eyes shut as I pieced together where I was and what had transpired over the last twenty-four hours. My mind was so clouded with medication and lack of sleep that I could not think rationally, and I was nearly consumed with anxiety. My heart racing, I was reluctant to open my eyes to my painful reality.

Finally, I slowly opened my eyes and saw Tony sitting in the chair next to me with his eyes shut. "Where is Steven?" I asked softly as I reached out and touched his arm.

"They still have him in recovery." He sat up from a slumped position in his chair and squeezed my hand as he looked at me. Neither of us said anything about Steven's diagnosis, but both of us had tears in our eyes as we looked at each other. *There are no words to express this...*

> *His heart is still broken. He will only live a day or two.*

We sat quietly for a few minutes before I broke the silence, "I don't know how I'm going to make it through this next week. I'm just not strong enough." In a matter of seconds, the tears became sobs as I felt the weight of what was to come.

Tony didn't have words to console me. We both cried until the nurse came in to check on us.

"When can we see Steven?" I anxiously asked through my tears.

"We will be taking you back to your room in a few minutes." She handed me a box of tissues. "Your son is not quite ready for a visit, but your family is still here, and they want to see you."

Looking at Tony, I asked, "Is it Mom and Dad?" I was no longer sobbing and was using the tissues to wipe my eyes.

The nurse cut him off before he could answer. "There is a whole lot more than just Mom and Dad. Last time I checked, there were around 20-25 people out there."

Tony nodded, "Your mother called everyone when you went into surgery. They have all been here for hours."

I smiled through the tears thinking about my entire family waiting for hours to see Steven and me. *I have an awesome family.*

About 9:00 p.m., I was able to go back to my room and visit with my family but still had not seen Steven. Finally, around 10:00 p.m., they brought him to us.

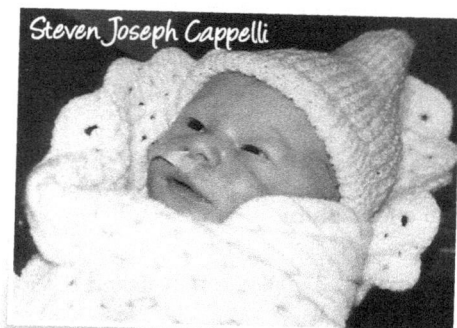

Wrapped up in a yellow and white blanket, his eyes were open. *What a beautiful boy!* After removing the tiny blue and white cap from his head, I could see that his hair was light brown and his eyes a dark blue that would surely turn brown like mine. After holding him for about ten minutes, I gave him to Tony, and before long, everyone was taking turns.

"I wonder if the miracle could still happen," I whispered to Grace who was sitting beside me, holding Steven. "He looks so healthy to me."

My entire family was able to stay in my hospital room and hold Steven. There were a lot of tears, but also joy as everyone spent time and took pictures with him. Tony was going to baptize him, but decided to have my mother do it so he could be closer to Steven and me.

The nurse brought us purified water in a small paper cup. As my mother poured a little of the water on Steven's head, I heard her whisper, "I baptize you in the name of the Father, the Son, and the Holy Spirit." It was a special moment for everyone. Tissues were being passed around, as there wasn't a dry eye in the room.

It was a very long day and night, and shortly after 11:00 p.m., everyone left. I enjoyed having my family with us, but it was nice to spend some alone-time with Steven and Tony. We took turns holding him until about midnight. We had decided that Tony would go home and come back in the morning, so we called the nurse to come and get Steven.

So tired and medicated, I could not appreciate the time with him and prayed as the nurse walked out with him. *Oh God, please let him live through the night so we can spend some quality time with him in the morning.*

A Day with My Angel
December 14

I woke up feeling a little rested and very excited to see Steven. The despair from the night before was gone, and I felt oddly at peace with the situation. Before they brought him to me, the NICU nurse came to check on me.

After some small talk, she asked, "What is your religious background?" She had a puzzled look on her face when she asked and looked away when our eyes met. She seemed a little uncomfortable to me.

Thinking it was a strange question, I answered, "I'm Catholic, but my mother has already baptized him." I was hoping she did not want a priest to visit me because I was not ready to talk to anyone about Steven's unhealed heart.

The nurse asked a few more questions regarding my faith and my relationship with God before she finally got to what was on her mind. "I have a strong feeling that Steven's heart condition is all part of a bigger plan. God's plan." She waited for my reaction, but my response was slow in coming.

"Until yesterday's echocardiogram, I would have agreed with you." Because I was not up to a long conversation, I debated on whether to give her details. After a brief hesitation, I decided to tell her a little about God's presence throughout the pregnancy, signs of a promise to come, and our hope that the promise would translate into Steven's heart healing.

About ten minutes later, I ended the conversation with, "I'm not sure if any of this matters. I don't care about God's big plan or promise for Steven if he dies." The peace I woke up with suddenly disappeared. I was becoming emotional and feeling sorry for myself, fighting back tears. There was an awkward pause while she finished folding the blanket. She was hesitant to continue, but I knew there was more she wanted to say. She moved closer to the bed before she spoke again.

"I truly believe there is more to His plan that will bring you hope and peace. God will get you through this." I think she wanted to say more, but probably sensed I wasn't up for it. I didn't ask her why she believed there was a bigger plan for Steven because, at the moment, I didn't care. It was just one more whisper from God involving hope and healing for Steven that made little sense to me. Only this time, it was coming from someone I didn't even know.

I changed the subject. "When will I be able to see Steven?" With nervous anticipation, I asked one more question: "Do you know how he is doing?"

"One of the other nurses is getting him ready to come see you right now. It should only be a few more minutes," she replied as she picked up a cup from the table next to me. She smiled and said, "In fact, I will go check on him now."

Before Steven was brought into the room, I received a call from Kim. "I'll be arriving from Colorado around 1:00 p.m. and will come straight to the hospital." There was a pause before she added, "I don't know what to think about Steven's heart." She was clearly shaken that Steven's heart condition remained in critical condition. Her voice was quiet and less confident than usual.

"That makes two of us."

We talked a little more about details from the night before when she asked, "Did your mom tell you what I shared with her while you were in surgery?"

"No, but I haven't had much time to talk to her alone. She will be coming to visit me in a few minutes."

Kim interrupted, "While you were having your surgery, I had a vision and called your mom. I was so sure Steven's heart would be healed because in the vision, Christ was in the operating room with you. He was working through your anesthesiologist who was leaning over you, stroking your face and calming you down."

I was speechless as I remembered the moments of comfort I had shared with the doctor in the operating room. At the time, his actions seemed unusually kind, but I was too panicked to think much beyond the moment. As Kim recalled details of her vision, I clearly remembered staring into the doctor's eyes and relaxing a little, despite the chaos happening around me. I also clearly remembered it was my anesthesiologist because we had spoken for a few minutes when he had administered the epidural earlier during the day.

Tony had also seen the doctor stroke my face in an effort to calm me down, but with all that has transpired, we never discussed it with each other, let alone anyone else. I was stunned to hear Kim relay the details exactly as they unfolded the night before. *How did Kim know it was the anesthesiologist?*

In shock, I was unable to respond to what I had just heard. Finally, she paused and asked, "Sandy, are you there?"

"I'm sorry, Kim." I was choked up and could barely speak. "It happened. Your vision was just as it happened in the operating room." We hung up before I had a chance to ask her how she knew it was my anesthesiologist who had comforted me.

> *I caressed his head and face and loosened the blanket so I could pull his tiny little arms and hands out. He is perfect.*

Shortly after my conversation with Kim, Tony walked in the room. Before I could tell him about Kim's vision, the nurse brought Steven to us, and Tony and I marveled at his beauty. I caressed his head and face and loosened the blanket so I could pull his tiny little arms and hands out. *He is perfect.*

The pain from the C-section made it difficult to cuddle him for long periods so Tony and I took turns holding him. My mother arrived about twenty minutes later, and after her, my family and friends arrived throughout the day. Videos and pictures were taken with everyone. In spite of the exhaustion, I really enjoyed seeing all of my favorite people holding my son.

My most memorable moment that day occurred when Nicolas and Alexa arrived at the hospital. Alexa was visiting with her aunties in my hospital room while Tony held Nicolas close to Steven.

"This is your little brother, Steven." Nicolas smiled and gently touched Steven's head. "Can you say hello to him?" Nicolas touched Steven's cheek with his finger, and then leaned over and put his lips on his head, giving him a big, wet kiss.

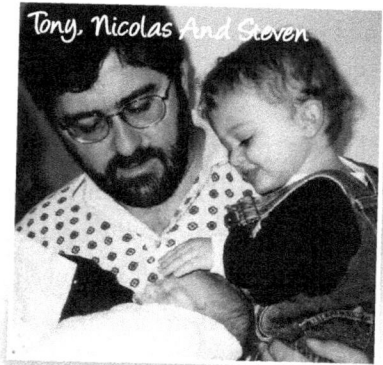

Tony, Nicolas And Steven

A few minutes later, we were all together, with Nicolas, Alexa, and Steven in the hospital bed with me, and Tony in the chair next to us. I truly felt joy as I watched my entire family together. *God, I still can't believe that your plan is to take our beautiful baby from us.* Even at that point in this long painful journey, it was easier to hope for the miracle than to face the reality of the situation.

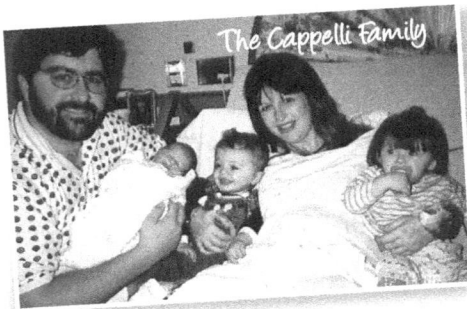

The Cappelli Family

Steven stayed with us in the room the entire day. The doctor visited and told me he was looking good, not showing signs of stress. "He will probably live a day or two, but you should consider the options in case he lives longer." Because it looked like we would have Steven another full day, Tony decided to go home and sleep at the house.

Jack, Kim, Carol & Steven

Mom, Dad & Steven

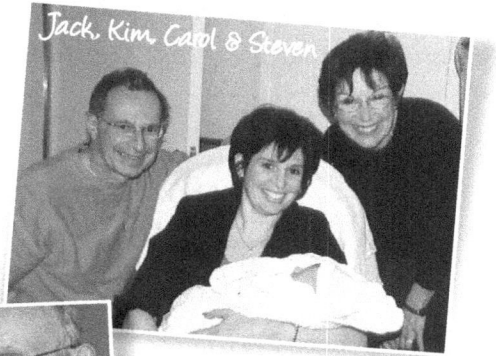

"I'll call you if there are any changes to Steven's condition," I promised Tony, as he was getting ready to leave.

"Okay. Try to get some rest." He kissed Steven and me on our foreheads before leaving.

"Drive safe." I gave his hand a squeeze. "I know how tired you are, so please be careful." He winked at me before walking out the door.

I didn't want Tony to go, but it was nice to spend some time with Steven alone. The nurse came in around 10:00 p.m. to check on us. "Go ahead and take him," I told her. "I want to rest so I can spend another good day with him." She reached to take him from my arms.

I didn't want to say it out loud, but I'm scared that if I keep him in here with me, he might die while I am sleeping.

Have you ever had a bittersweet moment — when you were experiencing the joy and pain at the same time?

Chapter 11

Losing Faith

"Therefore you now have sorrow; but I will see you again, and your heart will rejoice, and your joy no one will take from you."

~ John 16:22 NKJV ~

32 Hours
December 15

I was in a deep sleep when the nurse came in at 2:00 a.m. "Sandy," she whispered. It took only a second for me to shoot straight up in the bed. "You need to call your husband. Steven doesn't have much time."

Fumbling with the phone, I quickly dialed my home phone number and prayed Tony would not be in too deep of a sleep. He answered after the first ring. "Tony, you need to come now." I didn't try to hide the panic in my voice.

"I'll be right there."

As I hung up the phone, the nurse brought Steven to me. He was swaddled in a blanket and his eyes were closed. I held him close to me. He looked so peaceful, and although the lights were dim, I didn't notice a change in his color. I was alone with Steven humming "Amazing Grace" when Tony came in. He sat down beside me and cradled Steven's head. Neither Tony nor I were crying; we were just sitting close to each other with Steven between us.

We called my mother and Kim to let them know Steven was not expected to make it through the night. Mom quietly replied, "Honey, I want you to have your last moments with Steven alone. Call me if you need me." I could hear her voice quiver as she tried to be strong for me.

My aunt, uncle, and Kim were an hour away and asked to come to the hospital. "You are welcome to come, but I don't think Steven has an hour to live."

"We would like to come anyway," Kim whispered.

About a half hour after talking with Kim, the nurse walked in and checked Steven's pulse. His eyes were still shut. "It won't be much longer," she said quietly. "I'll be back in a few minutes."

"Lord, take care of our precious baby," I whispered.

Tony added, "You are our beautiful boy, and we will never forget you, Steven."

"Mommy and Daddy will always love you," I said with his head cradled in my arm. I rubbed his head, arm, and his tiny little fingers. After a couple of seconds, I leaned over and kissed his cheek for the last time.

> "Mommy and Daddy will always love you," I said with his head cradled in my arm. I rubbed his head, arm, and his tiny little fingers. After a couple of seconds, I leaned over and kissed his cheek for the last time.

Tears were rolling down our faces when two nurses walked in the room. One of them took his pulse and about thirty seconds later, while still taking his pulse, she said, "Time of death is 3:35 a.m." The other nurse wrote something on our chart. Both nurses stayed in the room as we cried with Steven still in our arms.

"Would you like me to take him now?" she asked after several minutes had passed.

"No, I need a little more time."

"Take as long as you want," she said before both nurses left us alone in our room.

Steven Joseph Cappelli had lived for thirty-two hours. When Kim walked through the door thirty minutes later, Steven was no longer in the room with us, but she somehow already knew. "He is gone, isn't he?" I nodded and she continued speaking. "On the way to the hospital, I had a vision. I saw a beautiful gold altar with steps leading up to it. At the top stood Jesus, and at the base, kneeling, were you and Tony. Steven was in your arms. Steven appeared to be three or four years old. He had blond curly hair, wiry little legs, and a very prominent Italian nose. He left your arms and ran up the stairs toward Jesus. Steven took hold of Jesus' hand and they walked away."

Kim paused for a few seconds and finished giving us the details of her vision. "Steven looked back at both of you, let go of Jesus' hand, and ran to give you one more hug. Then he walked up the stairs again. This time, I saw Grandpa standing behind the Lord. Grandpa appeared to be about fifty. He still had his round tummy and his pants pulled up too high like he always wore them. He was laughing and calling for Steven to come, and Steven ran and jumped into his arms. Grandpa squeezed his cheeks, and they both laughed. The three of them went off together." She took a breath before finishing. "When I opened my eyes from the vision, I asked my mother what time it was. It was 3:35 a.m. I knew Steven had gone home."

With a bittersweet smile at the thought of Steven with our grandfather, I closed my eyes to hold onto the image for a few seconds. I don't know why Steven was older in the vision and my grandfather was much younger than his ninety-six years, but it doesn't matter. The image is a small ray of light in what will be some very dark days ahead.

The rest of the day brought more visitors, more flowers, and more pain. *I can hardly believe my precious baby is gone.* I had several deep conversations with nurses on faith and the impact that Steven has had on so many of us. There were a lot of tears shed in that small room.

> *I can hardly believe my precious baby is gone.*

That first night without Steven in the hospital was painfully long. I could hardly sleep, with the screams of mothers in labor and the cries of newborn babies echoing in the hallways. I wrote a letter to God to pass the time and vent my hurt, anger, and pain.

> *Dear God,*
>
> *I am so very sad and confused today; I don't know whether to cry or scream, and most of my anger is directed toward You. I have so many questions left unanswered. Forgive my bluntness. Is this the magnificent day You have been promising me? And have you fulfilled Your promise to me? If You have, I think I need a clarification of what Your promise was, and why You thought I would find peace with it.*
>
> *After a long, painful pregnancy and a long, painful delivery, You blessed me with a child of my own flesh and blood for a day. Steven may be a blessing in my life, but asking me to rejoice and find peace in letting him go is more than I can bear. I have been taken to a new level of grief and heartache. In fact, heartbreak seems like a more accurate definition.*

What were all the signs, whispers, and excitement leading up to this painful day about? Why did You let me stray with so many confusing signs that a miracle of his physical healing might come? Why didn't You just let me grieve and accept the diagnosis back in August? I did not agree back then it was a blessing to carry a child for You and give him back in a day, but I did believe it was Your will. I truly believed You wanted me to have this child, Your child, even though it would be the most difficult and painful challenge of my life. In time, I might come to see our child as a blessing instead of a sacrifice.

Your signs confused not just me, but many of us. I may be new to Your ways of communicating signs and words, but people like Kim and Uncle Jack are not. How did they get so far from Your true plan? Why didn't You communicate a clearer message so that we didn't walk this journey with You under a complete misconception? I would have still walked the journey with You knowing Steven was going to die, but I would have been better prepared for the outcome and would have become a stronger person because of it.

Instead, I feel empty from the loss of my son, and foolish for having believed a miracle of this magnitude could have ever happened to me. I also hate the pity I sense from all the people with whom I shared my hopes of a miracle.

It has been barely twenty-four hours since Steven died, and it is probably too soon for me to be writing to You. I am still in the hospital recovering from the surgery, and my physical pain is almost as deep as my emotional pain. Even with my hospital door shut, I can hear the cries of the healthy infants just born. I wish I could hear Steven's cry. It is 2:00 a.m., and my eyes are so swollen from the volume of tears I have cried, I can barely focus to write these words. The nurse just came to give me more pain pills, so maybe I will sleep. She doesn't know I take the pills for my broken heart and not my physical pain.

Lord, I do know You have been with me this whole time. I know that even with the incredible depth of my pain, You are bringing me strength to get through each day. I ask that You continue to bring me strength, especially through the difficult days ahead of me. I am truly sorry I don't feel this was as great of a plan as You do. Just help me to accept it for now, and maybe with time, I will think differently.

From the time of the heart diagnosis, I have prayed for answers – a reason that would make some sense to me. Steven wasn't large enough to donate his organs, so his death won't even be able to help other children. It all seems so pointless. So far, I have no answers, no reasons, and no peace. Please give me this much.

I don't know whether to cry or scream, and most of my anger is directed toward You. I have so many questions left unanswered. Forgive my bluntness. Is this the magnificent day You have been promising me?

Arrangements
December 16

By the morning, I was very ready to leave the hospital. After an incredibly long night, Tony picked me up around 9:30 a.m. The numbness and pain medications were wearing off, and the physical pain and emotional grief were setting in. I knew if I didn't get home to the twins soon, I might have a meltdown in the hospital.

From the hospital, we went with my mother to the mortuary to make the final arrangements. The funeral was planned for Wednesday the twentieth at Forest Lawn Cemetery in Covina, California.

I remembered the day in October when my mother and I made tentative funeral arrangements, hoping we would not need to carry them out. I couldn't help but think about the young woman at the gravesite of her stillborn child. I remembered how my heart ached for her that day. *Today, my heart aches for me.*

After leaving the cemetery, we went home to our beautiful babies, who will continue to bring enormous comfort to my soul. But the void from the beautiful baby we left behind is unshakable. Family and friends might fill the void for the short term, but I know the road ahead is going to be a difficult one.

Looking for Answers
December 17

I feel so much pain. I'm taking a lot of pain medication and anxiety pills when breathing becomes difficult, which happens frequently.

Uncle Jack and Aunt Carol visited me today. They wanted to see how I was doing and to discuss the details of Steven's funeral, which Uncle Jack will be officiating. We were sitting in the family room and Nicolas and Alexa were playing on the floor with a toy that popped noisily as they dragged it across the carpet when Uncle Jack started with the conversation that was weighing heavily on our minds, "Sandy, I know the pain you must be feeling, but I still believe God's promise for Steven is yet to come."

By the time he finished the sentence, tears were streaming down my face. I was silent for several seconds before asking, "How can you possibly believe the promise is still to come? My child is dead." I wasn't trying to make him feel bad, but his statement made no sense to me.

Although Uncle Jack is very sad that Steven passed away, his faith seems unshaken. After a moment, he carefully answered my question, "I believe His promise was one of power, to reveal Himself to us, and to promise us a

> "I'm glad he has not lost his faith, but I'm afraid I have lost mine."

miracle of healing. God showed His power and revealed Himself to us on many occasions, but His promise of a miracle and healing have not yet happened."

"What does that mean? Steven is dead; who is left to heal?" Emotional, but not angry, I was speaking softly with tears in my eyes. Alexa saw me crying and dashed to the box of tissues on the table across the room. She ran back to where I was sitting and tried to wipe my nose and eyes with it. I gave her a hug and kissed her on her cheek before she scurried off to play with Nicolas.

Uncle Jack's answer was vague. "I don't believe God would waste His time or our faith with signs of hope for healing if there wasn't a good reason for doing so. I believe something big will come of Steven's short life."

In his mind, there is no question that God communicated signs to us over the past nine months. It was the *interpretation* of God's words that leaves us with so many questions.

I'm glad he has not lost his faith, but I'm afraid I have lost mine.

A Final Visit
December 19

Today is Tony's birthday – and the day before Steven will be laid to rest. We took the kids to the babysitter's house so we could spend some time together and do a little Christmas shopping. We also went by the mortuary with my mom and Grace to see Steven for the last time, and to make sure everything was ready for the service. *I don't know how I am going to get through tomorrow.*

When we arrived, I wasn't sure if I was mentally prepared to see Steven's lifeless body, but before we left, I decided to look at my beautiful baby one more time. I was surprised at how peaceful he appeared lying in his white casket, wearing the baby blue velour outfit my mother had bought him a few weeks ago. He looked like he was sleeping.

My little angel, how I wish you were just sleeping.

Have you ever lost your faith?

Chapter 12

Goodbye, For Now

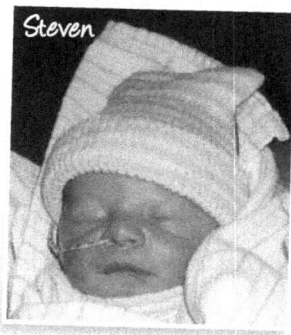

Steven

"And God will wipe away
every tear from their eyes;
there shall be no more death,
nor sorrow, nor crying.
There shall be no more pain,
for the former things
have passed away."

~ Revelation 21:4 NKJV ~

Goodbye, My Sweet Child
December 20

A pain pill, an anxiety pill, and a quick prayer was what I hoped would get me through the day without falling apart. *For some reason, I don't want to show my grief to the world.* Tony and I didn't have much to say to each other. I was still moving slowly from the surgery, and it had taken longer than usual to get the kids and myself ready.

After I got the kids dressed, Tony took them downstairs to give me some time to get ready. I had music on, but was feeling dysfunctional from the anxiety medication. *Should I even bother with the makeup?* I sat in front of my vanity mirror, dreading what I knew was coming. I put three pairs of pants on before deciding. Nothing was fitting, as my maternity pants were too big and my regular ones were too small. I knew Tony was getting restless downstairs, concerned we would be late, but I didn't really care. *They can't start the service without us, right?*

Once in the car, Tony reached over and put his hand on my arm to break the silence. "Are you sure you're okay? You haven't said much today."

"I guess I've been talking to God more than to you," I stared out the window. "I told God it wasn't too late for Him to show up and bring life to my sweet child."

There was a long silence before Tony answered. "That would be fine, although we would surely lose some family and friends to heart attacks." He has a way of putting things into perspective.

But I am desperate to hold on a little longer. I'm not ready to part with my baby who was so alive inside of me for the past nine months. I'm not ready for his life to be over. How do I get ready? Oh God, please help me to get ready.

"I hope I don't fall apart today. You are handling this a lot better than I am," I mumbled quietly and continued to stare out the window.

"I hope I don't fall apart today."

"We will get through this together," Tony assured me as he turned the car into the parking lot of Forest Lawn Cemetery. He reached across the seat to hold my hand. Alexa must have seen him because, out of the corner of my eye, I saw her reach out and hold Nicolas' hand.

"We need a happy thought to remember if we start feeling too emotional," I said as I tried desperately to think of a happy thought.

"I've got it." I said in a soft voice while unbuckling my seatbelt. "You know how Alexa made the association that tissues are for runny noses and has been running around wiping everyone's nose?" Tony nodded before I continued. "If we get too emotional, we will think about that and our 'code' will be to rub the bottom of our nose with our finger."

Tony smiled, but didn't comment as he pulled Nicolas out of his car seat. I glanced in the direction of the chapel and winced at the sight of our family and friends walking in. "I'm just not ready to talk to anybody." *And I don't want to see my baby's casket.* "I'm going to find someplace to hide."

"There should be a room on the side of the chapel. Go over to the side entrance and see if it's locked," he said, taking Alexa from my arms. He walked off with a kid in each arm. I headed in the direction he pointed.

"If you see Mom, ask her to come find me. I could use some company right now." I was fighting back tears.

Within a couple of minutes, my mom was at my side, holding my hand. I could see she was fighting back tears as well, so I decided not to talk to her. *We will both break down if we try to speak.*

The service was at 9:00 a.m. From where I was waiting in the small room, I could not see inside the chapel, so I had no idea of who had shown up for the service. I assumed it would only be family and a few close friends. Tony and the kids entered with Uncle Jack, who asked if we wanted to enter through the back of the chapel or the side entrance, which was a short distance from the front row we would be sitting in.

For the sake of ease, and because I didn't want the attention of walking down the center aisle, I chose the side entrance. My mom had already taken her seat, so Tony picked up Alexa, and I held Nicolas' hand as we walked out of the room. I was stunned when I saw the inside of the chapel packed with people. We walked over to Grace and passed off the twins to her and my sister and then took our seats.

Uncle Jack's opening prayer expressed some of the confusion, emptiness, and frustration I had been feeling:

"O Lord, we come here today to remember and to celebrate the short but very special life of Steven Joseph Cappelli. Our hearts feel hollow and empty. His light was with us for such a brief moment. Father, we thank you that we did have a second to hold him, to experience him, and to love him; and, while we wish it would have been many days, Lord, we accept your dominion and your will. Please strengthen us in our grief, fill us in our void, and build us in our faith. Forgive us for our questions and frustrations, and help us to see the light of your plan and your love."

His opening prayer only validated the questions swarming in my head. *I just want to know, Lord. Why? Why did you make this promise?*

I reached over and put my hand on Tony's leg, and he put his over mine and gave it a squeeze. I heard a shuffle as I looked over to see Alexa being passed to my sister while Grace walked up to the podium to read the beautiful poem she had written for Steven:

We only knew you for a day
that barely gave us time to say
how much we love you,
want to hold you,
want to hug you, get to know you.
Your beautiful face, like sunshine beamed.
Your touch so precious, and it seemed
we'd have a lifetime to enjoy

this gift from Heaven,
this baby boy.
But God in all His glory cried
to have this baby by His side,
so He could love him,
get to hold him,
let angels hug him, get to know him.
How very special you must be
God spoke of you triumphantly,
of beating death
and living life,
a life beyond our earthly strife.
So Steven, now you rest in Heaven.
Your heart is whole, your breathing even.
A little angel filled with joy,
Our gift to Heaven
This brave little boy.
You touched our lives in such a way
We'll always know you for a day.

I was trying to hold myself together, but tears were spilling from my eyes. Hearing the sobs from people around me only made me sadder. I looked away from Grace because it was too hard for me to see her so broken as she read her beautiful poem.

How are we all going to get through this?

After Grace's poem, Uncle Jack read the eulogy that he had written for Steven. He began by reading the opening verses from the Book of First Samuel in the Old Testament and then related it back to some of the trials that we have in common to the scripture:

"These are the opening verses from the Book of First Samuel in the Old Testament, and they discuss the turmoil of a mother named Hannah, who was unable to bear a child. She finally promised God that if he would give her a son, she would dedicate the boy to his service for all of his days. The son she bore was Samuel, the great prophet whom God used to establish the founding of Israel, and eventually to anoint David as King…"

I took a deep breath when I realized where he was going.

"…We are here today to share about another son, whose mother was also unable to conceive, and yet whom God gave both a beautiful set of twins as well as a special boy, named Steven Joseph. Steven was born on Wednesday night, December 13th at about 7:00 p.m. He was called home to heaven by God on Friday morning, December 15th at 3:35 a.m. His total time on earth outside the womb was just thirty-two hours…"

I closed my eyes as Uncle Jack spoke. *Thirty-two hours. Such a short time, Lord. Why so little time?*

"…Just as Samuel was given over to the service of God while still a baby, Steven Joseph was called to be with the Lord just hours after his birth. And just as Samuel made a profound impact on the history of the world by his years on earth, I believe Steven is destined to make an impact on this world long after his short visitation here…"

It didn't make sense. *How can he make a difference? He wasn't here long enough to make a difference!*

"…Steven's story begins a few months after the birth of Alexa and Nicolas, Tony and Sandy's twins. Although Sandy has a condition that rendered her unable to conceive without medical intervention, she soon found herself pregnant without the aid of medical science. After some questioning of themselves about how they were going to handle three small children, Sandy and Tony's joy over the prospect of another child overcame any concerns…"

God gave me so much peace. Why did I think everything would be okay?

"…Their joy was severely tested in August when they found out that Steven had a serious heart problem. Their first concern was the prospect of a Down Syndrome child, but that concern was soon overshadowed by the reality that Steven Joseph had an incurable and always-fatal heart malformation…"

That was a horrible day…

"…It was about this same time that God started speaking to Sandy and Tony about the special character of this child. Sandy and Tony had to deal with their own frailties and ask whether they could handle Sandy's carrying the baby to term, knowing that he was destined to die. Yet God seemed to be asking them to trust Him, both for His miraculous power and to know what was best for Steven and for them…"

Once again, I found myself in prayer, bowing my head and clasping my hands. *Was that really Your will, Lord?*

"…Some of us believed this meant that God planned to heal Steven in a miraculous manner somewhere along the way. God gave various dreams, signs, and visions to Sandy and Tony and to others who are close to them to confirm the word that was being spoken to them. The message was always one of power, one of healing, and one of trust – that He is in control of the lives of those who entrust themselves to Him, and this clearly included Steven…"

Was that really Your will, Lord?

I thought You were going to heal him.

"…Against medical advice, Sandy and Tony made the courageous decision to complete the pregnancy and trust God for the result, hoping that God would work a miracle and heal Steven of this condition. Well, God has worked a miracle; He has demonstrated His power, but He did not heal Steven of his heart problem. A few of us were privileged to hold Steven and experience his presence during his few hours here. As you can see from his picture, he was a beautiful and precious child here on earth and he is now a radiant child of the King in heaven…"

I thought about that vision Kim had of him grabbing Jesus' hand. *Yes, my radiant son.*

"…Of course, in heaven, Steven has been healed of his heart malformation. He certainly has no need for the faulty heart he left behind; but I believe that the healing God promised is yet to come. No, I don't expect Steven to come back in some way; he is much too happy now in the eternal presence of the Lord. But I do believe the faith and power that were brought to bear in his birth will bring forth healing and fruit for the kingdom of God. Jesus said, 'Unless a kernel of wheat falls to the ground and dies, it remains a single seed. But if it dies, it produces many seeds. The man who loves his life will lose it, while he who gives it up in this world will keep it in eternal life…'"

What seeds, Lord? Show me the purpose of all of this.

"…We do not know the manner God has chosen to fulfill His ultimate plan. It could come about in a variety of ways. It might be through the book Sandy has written that chronicles her journey of faith; it might be in the telling of the story by any one of us; or it might be in a mysterious way that only God can imagine. But I do know that God does not waste anything. He does not waste our prayers, He does not waste our love, He does not waste our faith, and He does not waste the life of a precious child like Steven Joseph…"

I leaned into Tony's arm. As we held hands, I thought about how much I am going to miss hearing my son's name.

Steven Joseph, I love you, and I will never forget you. You will never be a waste to me…

"…God promised a miracle through the birth and life of Steven. We thought it would manifest in the physical healing of his heart, but we were wrong. Our desires, our prayers, and our dreams were much too small for the hand of God. Just as no one could have guessed that the insignificant child whom Hannah left behind at the temple that day would be instrumental in changing the course of history, so no one can guess how God will honor the faith and love of Sandy and Tony in giving up their precious son, Steven, to the hands of the Lord."

With my attention span so short, I was surprised how focused I remained during the entire eulogy. I was feeling the emotion of every word, and although choked up, I held back tears as best as I could.

After Uncle Jack's eulogy, my mother walked up to the podium to read the letter she had written for Steven. As she headed up the aisle, I heard another scuffle as Nicolas started running after her yelling "Nana" and my niece went running after him. He protested as she scooped him up and headed to the side of the chapel and quieted him with some cookies. *Ah yes. The cookie bribe. It works every time.*

As my mom read her letter, my heart broke even more. I've always struggled with her pain.

"Little grandson, you lived your lifetime in a few short hours, but, oh, the love you brought to us all. We looked so forward to meeting you and holding you close. Your mother wanted you so badly. She chose life for you, not knowing what to expect. You were such a joy to her all of those months she carried you. She loved you so much. Your dad had so much love and hope for you. Nicolas and Alexa, your big brother and sister, were going to be your protectors. Now you are our little angel in heaven. Now you will be watching over all of us…"

I was squeezing Tony's hand so tightly as she read her letter, he glanced down at me and whispered, "Are you okay?" I nodded without saying a word. *Barely.* I knew how hard it was for my mother to be up there sharing her thoughts, and I found myself so consumed with grief for her that I was almost faint. *How I wish I could take your pain away, my sweet mother.*

"…So many of us were looking forward to your birth, your grandparents, all of your aunts and uncles and cousins, friends. There was so much love waiting for you. We had such plans for you – but God had a greater plan – and now you have a greater life. Someday, maybe, we will understand all of this…"

God, please help us to understand.

"…I know you have one of the most wonderful mothers in the world. I was wishing you had gotten to know her better, but, somehow, I am sure you know her – her thoughts, her heart, her soul. I know how much your mom and dad love you, and how heartbreaking it was for them to see you go. I know how much they wanted you. We all wanted you…"

Yes, sweet child of mine. We still want you.

"…And so, goodbye for now, our sweet little boy. We will meet another time, in another life, where all is good, and there is only love. For now, know that we will never forget you. We will always have you in our hearts."

By the time she finished, tears were falling down my face, and I heard others in the room sniffling and blowing their noses. I smiled through the tears as she walked over and hugged me before sitting back down next to my dad.

I hit the jackpot when it comes to mothers.

Next, a beautiful and touching poem entitled *"This Side of Heaven"* by Jan McIntosh was read by my niece.

This Side Of Heaven

This side of Heaven
It's sometimes hard to see
The blessings he has waiting
On the other side for me.

I don't always understand
His methods or His plan.
I can only walk by faith,
While clinging to His hand.
Someday He'll lift the veil
And these poor eyes will see
Beyond the clouded visions
To reveal His mysteries.
For now, I can only wait,
While trusting in His plan.
'Til I leave this side of Heaven
And enter the Promised Land.

Waiting until I leave this side of heaven and enter the Promised Land…
That's too long. I want to know why…now…

We concluded the service with everyone singing "Amazing Grace" which lifted my spirits a little. I looked over to see tears streaming down Tony's face and touched the bottom of his nose to remind him of the happy thought involving Alexa and the tissues. We looked over at Nicolas and Alexa who were sitting with Grace, eating cookies and loudly chattering nonsense to each other, and we both managed a smile.

I've been so consumed with my own pain, I've hardly thought about his pain. I need to support him, but I wish I felt stronger.

There were around 125 people at the service and more cars than I had ever seen in a funeral procession driving to the gravesite. *All for our Steven.*

The gravesite was at the top of a hill, and I was so weak that I could barely walk up the steep incline. My dad and my brother-in-law came alongside me and helped me get to the gravesite. We were following Tony's brother and my Uncle, who were both carrying the casket with Steven in it. Most of the funeral attendees slowly made their way up the hill. I was worried about my father-in-law, who could barely walk on his own, and was relieved to see other family members helping him along.

I looked over my shoulder when I heard Tony call out to Nicolas. "Nicolas, come back here, now." Nicolas, squealing with delight, was running away from Tony, who was trying to guide him up the hill.

"I'll get him," my niece yelled back as she went chasing after him. Nicolas was so fast that he was already way ahead of her. He shrieked when she finally caught him and twirled him around in circles a couple of times. His laughter in the midst of the somber environment was refreshing, and I caught myself smiling as Tony impatiently waited for my niece to bring Nicolas back.

Within seconds, I heard another scuffle and my cousin pleading with Alexa: "Don't take those, Alexa. They are not yours." I followed the voice in the opposite direction of Nicolas to see Alexa holding flowers she had picked up from a grave. There was a short scream in protest from Alexa as my cousin tried to pry the flowers out of her tight grip. Grace walked over to her with a box of animal crackers, and within seconds, she was stuffing crackers in her mouth. *Never a dull moment.*

Once everyone had made it up the hill, we said our final goodbyes. After Uncle Jack said a few words, we all released white balloons. My sister handed out small toy trucks and cars, instead of the typical rose, for people to put on the casket while saying their final goodbyes. Nicolas was fascinated with the toys and immediately squirmed out of my mom's arms to run to the casket, grabbing a toy truck for each hand. *Oh Nicolas, I am so glad you don't know your baby brother is in that box beneath those toys.*

"Goodbye, Little Buddy."

Alexa saw everyone putting something on the casket, so she threw her pacifier next to the toys to show her support. Without missing a beat, Nicolas seized her pacifier and stuck it in his mouth. I grabbed Nicolas' shirt as he tried to walk past me, pulling him toward me before he caused any more distractions.

I was standing next to Tony holding Nicolas' arm when Tony reached out and put his hand on the casket. I heard him whisper, "Goodbye, Little Buddy." I slipped my hand into his other hand and gave it a squeeze.

I closed my eyes and looked up toward the heavens with tears streaming down my face. *I'm not ready to say goodbye because I'm not ready for Steven to be over. Maybe I won't say a final goodbye. I will say something less permanent…*

Goodbye, for now, my sweet child.

When, in your life, have you realized that you were stronger than you thought?

Chapter 13

Forever Different

"*For as the heavens are higher than the earth, so are My ways higher than your ways, and My thoughts than your thoughts.*"

~ Isaiah 55:9 NKJV ~

Where Do I Go From Here?
December 23

It has been three days since the funeral and eight days since Steven died. *These last three…these were the worst days of my life.* I guess there was so much going on from the time Steven was born to the time of his funeral that I didn't get a chance to really feel all that has happened.

These past few days I have had a lot of time – *too much time* – to reflect. Although I'm not taking medication for pain anymore, I do need an occasional pill for my anxiety. I am crying all the time and hoping some of the tears are just the hormones from the pregnancy. *Maybe things will look brighter by the first of the year?*

Today, I watched Tony bolt from one room to another, chasing after the kids, and wondered if he has had a chance to grieve. There is so much stress taking care of the twins and me.

"Do you think we should go to grief counseling? The hospital gave me information before we left." I was talking quietly because Nicolas had just fallen asleep in my arms.

"If you want to." He was reading the paper and did not show any change in his facial expression.

"Do you think you can benefit from it?" I laid Nicolas on a blanket in the family room and looked up into my husband's face.

"I don't think I need it," he said, "but if it will help you with your depression, I will go with you." He folded the paper, set it on the table next to his chair, and looked at me with very tired eyes. *The past few weeks have aged both of us.*

"How come you are handling this so much better than me?" Knowing the answer, I asked the question anyway. *He has been preparing for this for four months because he never believed that Steven would live.*

"It is painful for me too, but I know Steven is in a better place." He still did not show much emotion.

"I wish I could feel the peace you seem to be finding," I mumbled as I got up from the floor next to sleeping Nicolas. "I will consider counseling after the first of the year if life is still feeling as empty and bleak as it is now."

"I think it is a good idea." He paused, not wanting to upset me further. "I haven't seen you smile or laugh for a long time. I really do want to go with you if you'll go." I didn't answer as I headed up the stairs to our bedroom.

Sitting on our bed, I began thinking about my life. I am very blessed with a wonderful family, but I ache so much from the absence of Steven. I worry that I won't be able to move forward with life. Everyone around me is moving on, and I am still clinging to a past that includes Steven.

It is hard for me to see people laughing and doing normal everyday activities. Things that are important to them seem so unimportant to me. My normal is gone, and I feel lost. I can't describe the desperate feelings of pain, confusion, and anger. Words fail me. Less than two weeks ago, I was so excited and hopeful that my life would include the child that was full of life inside of me.

I don't even feel like praying right now. Prayers will not bring Steven back.

Today, that hope is gone. Steven is gone. My spirit is gone. I should be seeking God's help more than I am. I don't even feel like praying right now. Prayers will not bring Steven back.

A Promise to Come?
December 26

It has been eleven days since Steven died. I am doing a little better, I think. Although I haven't needed the anxiety or pain pills for a few days, I'm still having trouble sleeping. The emptiness is overwhelming at times. *How I wish I could feel Steven's kicks!* The holidays passed without me having any major meltdowns. Just a few tears fell with painful reminders of my precious son.

The hardest moments were in church on Christmas Eve. During my pregnancy, I didn't allow myself to mentally "bring Steven home," but I did treasure an image of the five of us at church on Christmas Eve. *This was where we spent some of our special moments. I felt so close to him during church services.* I was unable to focus on anything but Steven as I stared at the rainbow in the stained-glass window.

One of the happier moments on Christmas Day was when my sister, Lori, surprised us with a special gift. It was a framed and matted picture of the twins dressed in old-time attire. She must have had the photos taken when I left the kids with her before Steven's birth.

Both were wearing hats, and they had amusing expressions on their faces. Nicolas was wearing a tie and holding a rose, while Alexa was wearing several strands of beads around her neck. With all the frilly lace and beads, I'm sure she was in her "happy place." The picture was especially sentimental since I was unable to get the kids to sit still for Christmas pictures.

Nicolas & Alexa

All of my family and friends have been very supportive throughout the entire journey. They check up on me a lot more lately, probably concerned that I might go off the deep end. Terri stopped by this morning, and I found myself expressing a lot of emotion about my emptiness. "People don't call me at all, or when they do, they don't talk about Steven… and it hurts." I wiped a tear from my face.

"It is hard for people to know what to say to you."

"*I* don't even know what to say to me. Talking about Steven makes me cry. Not talking about Steven makes me cry. But I still want people to say something. The silence of people not knowing what to say is breaking my heart. I want people to acknowledge that Steven lived. I will always want people to acknowledge that he is my son."

"You can't be upset at people around you." She got up and poured herself another cup of coffee. "Everybody grieves differently, and that's why people don't know what to say. I'm sure they don't want to bring you more pain, so they avoid talking to you about Steven."

"I'm not ready to move on without him, but I find myself not wanting the people around me to move on either. I even bought these angel ornaments for you and all of my family with Steven's name engraved on them." Handing her the ornament I had engraved for her, I continued, "I don't want Steven forgotten, and I know people will at least think of him when they put their Christmas tree up each year." Terri thanked me for the ornament before I asked, "Why am I so concerned about people forgetting Steven?"

"Because he is so important to you." She reached out and put her hand on my arm.

"Yeah, and thirty-two hours just wasn't long enough for him to make a difference." There were a couple of seconds of silence before I quietly finished my thought. "It wasn't enough time for him to really impact the lives of people around me."

Unsure how to answer, Terri changed the topic of conversation, "By the way, how is Kim doing? Have you heard from her lately?"

"I got an email from her a few days ago. She received a 'word' a couple of days before, but was so depressed she didn't want to send it to me. She felt physically ill from refusing to send it, and after receiving the exact same 'word' three days later, she decided to pass it on to me. She made it clear she did not want to offer any interpretation."

"I have a plan that is to be revealed...I did not lead you astray...."

I walked over to my computer, and picked up a piece of paper with the words she had heard. "I sense Kim is shutting God out more than I am, and it really makes me sad...I think we both feel responsible for each other's pain right now," I said, as I handed Terri the paper. "When Kim sent it, she reminded me that she doesn't always understand what God tells her because it is not for her. She just writes what she hears."

"Why do you feel I have failed you? I am here. I am still here. I know you do not understand...but...I have a plan that is to be revealed...I did not lead you astray...As you cry out in the quiet of the night, I have heard your cries of pain and felt your suffering. I will, My child, bring about peace and rest in your house...Do not feel as if I have abandoned you in the desert, left you searching and getting no answers...Rest now in my arms of peace. I will hold you as you grieve your loss. I do know the depths of your pain. The day of promise is coming. Rest in My arms of peace. For I have not forsaken you."

"What do you think about it?" she asked.

"I think Kim is usually accurate in her interpretations, and this experience has caused her to lose confidence. This experience will bring caution to all of us."

"This latest word seems to indicate more to come," Terri said as she handed the paper back to me.

"I don't even want to think about a 'wonderful promise to come' with Steven dead. Even if I do figure out His promise for Steven, I doubt I will ever think it is wonderful." I didn't try very hard to hide the sarcasm in my voice.

Terri stayed a couple of hours and left shortly after the kids woke from their naps. After she was gone, I reread the word Kim had sent and cried some more. I focused on the sentence *"I did not lead you astray."*

That is what I wrote in my letter to God the night Steven died, "Why did you lead us astray…?"

Are you answering my plea, Lord?

I hope that if there really is a promise to come, it will bring joy and not more suffering to my family and me. It is in suffering that people build character and truly get to know God, but quite honestly, I don't want more suffering. From depression to infertility to the death of my son, the past several years have not been easy ones.

Life Goes On
December 30

Our neighbor gave birth to a healthy baby boy yesterday. As I watched the hustle and bustle of family and friends in and out of their house, I found myself overwhelmed with sadness once again. *I wish we could have had that kind of excitement at our house a couple of weeks ago.*

I threw out all the flowers because they are just painful reminders. Sympathy cards remain unopened. My feelings are very conflicted, and I just want to escape the grief.

It has been over two weeks since I've laughed. For a person who had at least one good belly laugh a day, that is a long time to be sad. Humor has always gotten me through difficult times, but nothing seems funny anymore. Overwhelmed with sadness, there are still times where I can't breathe. It is strange that only one year ago at Christmas, I was as happy as I have ever been. My twins were four months old, and we were celebrating our first Christmas together as the family I always dreamed of. And now I feel such emptiness.

God, I miss Steven.

Grace and I visited a few minutes today. We haven't talked much since Steven's death. She gave me a CD and card. Inside the card she wrote:

Dear Sandy,

There are several songs on this CD by Lee Ann Womack that I like, but the second one is my favorite. It's called 'I Hope You Dance.' I was thinking of you the other day when I heard it because I don't know anyone who has done more 'dancing' in her life. I have always admired you for that. I know you're having trouble right now finding any reason to dance – I'm sure your sadness is overwhelming. But when you're ready, I hope this song helps. And when you're ready, I hope I can be there to watch you dance.

Love, Grace

In the past, our conversations had always been so uplifting, but today we just cried. It is good to know someone is as confused as I am. Like me, she is still holding on for more. I read her the word Kim sent on December 24. It brought her some peace as it initially did me. She also wants to believe a promise is still to come.

"Do you pray much?" she asked.

"Not as much as I should," I answered. "I'm really struggling with my relationship with God right now. I know more than ever that He is the Master Architect of our lives, but I've lost confidence in my relationship with Him. I felt closer than I've ever felt to God these past four months, but now I'm not sure what was real about my spiritual growth during that time."

I thought Grace might try to redirect my thought process, but she listened silently without saying anything, so I let the flood of emotion pour out of me. "I'm not sure when God was truly leading me, and when it was my own spirit. Why did I believe Steven would be healed? Why did I feel I should share his story with so many people? Why did I feel compelled to write? And because I don't trust my judgment in what God is communicating to me anymore, I feel a little lost. It is a very empty feeling. I lost my son, and now I feel as though I have lost my God."

Grace replied, but her short response convinced me she was struggling with the same issues. "Don't give up on God, Sandy. I know He will get us through this."

Although I know she is right about leaning on God, I don't feel ready. I've been reading books on grief, but a large part of the grieving process involves talking and remembering the deceased. *I don't have much to remember.*

With so few memories, why do I hurt so badly? The lack of time and memories with Steven bring even more questions. His hands were big and his fingers were long, but I don't remember his legs and feet at all. I remember the curve of his nose and lips, but I never got to count his toes or kiss his belly. I wonder what his personality would be like, and if he would look like me.

God, I wish I had another day to check out his toes and feet and kiss his belly.

Who am I kidding? I wish I had another 10,000 days with him.

Answers of Sorts
January 1

It is a new year, and I am desperately trying to come to terms with the end of a huge chapter of my life; nine months and thirty-two hours of Steven. It is the beginning of a new year and the end of a really difficult one. From Alexa in the hospital the first week of last year to burying our son during the last, I am ready for a new year to begin.

> God made His presence known so many times that I'm convinced there is more to Steven's purpose...

If I am going to speed up the grieving process, I need to refocus my thoughts. I'm starting a list of peaceful thoughts that involve Steven – things that make me feel better. When the doubt and despair creep in, I will look at this list and find peace.

- God had a plan for Steven before he was conceived. Although I can't comprehend it all, there is a reason for Steven.

- I told God I would carry His child knowing he was destined to die shortly after birth. Steven was His child to take, and I made a promise to carry him, knowing we would not be able to keep him. And I would do it again today.

- God made His presence known so many times that I'm convinced there is more to Steven's purpose – a bigger promise to come. The last verse of the poem read at the funeral keeps coming back to me:

For now, I can only wait,
While trusting in His plan.
'Til I leave this side of Heaven
And enter the Promised Land.

- The idea of having Steven waiting for me in heaven when I die will make parting from this world a lot easier.
- Kim's vision of Steven with Grandpa brings me peace. God and Grandpa will take care of my son.
- I have faith that will get me through this.
- I have three children. *I will always have three children.*

Healing
January 15 – 1 Month

It has been one month since Steven died. For a solid month, I have grieved the loss of my precious son, but I am encouraged that thirty-one days have gone by, and I am surviving. How? *One day at a time.*

Imagining that I will never hold my baby again is too overwhelming a thought, but one day at a time seems to be working. I won't get to hold Steven in this lifetime, but one day, we will meet again.

I've been thinking more about Steven's grave marker and what to put on it. We need to do something, but I sense Tony doesn't want to address the issue. I don't know if it is because it makes him sad or because he knows it makes me sad. There is nothing more final than a name engraved on a headstone.

The days are starting to go by faster, so the healing process has begun. Very slowly, but nonetheless, it has begun. After a couple of good days in a row, I thought I was making real progress. Last Thursday, I actually got through the day without shedding a tear. I went to bed thinking *I can do this. I can get through this and be a stronger person because of it.* Friday brought a few tears, but I still had hope for light at the end of the tunnel. Saturday, I struggled a little more than Friday, and on Sunday, I had another complete meltdown. I couldn't stop sobbing, and was barely functional. Tony took the kids to visit his dad to give me a little space, but the empty house only added to my depression.

Grieving is a frustrating process. There may be ways to speed it up, but there is no escaping it. Denial won't work. *I can run, but I can't hide. So I will continue to let myself grieve for however long it takes.*

I will never regret having fulfilled God's will by giving Steven life, but I wonder how much I have personally benefitted from having given birth to Steven. *It is a selfish thought, but does the good outweigh the incredible grief I have suffered? Was Steven God's blessing to me, or my sacrifice for Him? More specifically, did I do this for God, or did God do this for me?* Faith can be so confusing.

I hope that one day I will know, without a doubt, what the good of this was – for God, for Steven, and for me. I want to believe in my heart, rather than convince myself, that Steven is a true blessing in my life. I long for the time when the mention of Steven's name brings a smile instead of tears – joy instead of pain. *I want an understanding of God's promise for Steven.*

Next month, I hope for fewer tears. At some point, there will be more happy days than sad ones. Eventually, there will just be sad moments instead of sad days. Although life will never get back to "normal," things will get better. *I wonder what the definition of normal is anyway?* I've decided to quit looking for things to get back to normal, and I am trying to find peace in "different."

I am forever different. Life after Steven will be forever different.

How have you had to let go of normal
and embrace "forever different?"

Chapter 14

Emerging Hope

"But those who hope in the Lord will renew their strength. They will soar on wings like eagles; they will run and not grow weary, they will walk and not be faint."

~ Isaiah 40:31 NIV ~

Faith
February 15 – 2 Months

It has been thirty days since I last sat down to write, and sixty days since Steven died. The past month has been difficult at times, although much better than the last one. As a way to keep Steven a big part of my life, I hung pictures of him in every room. The one in the living room hangs next to a colorful picture that my sister, Lori, gave me shortly after Steven died. It says, "God danced the day you were born."

I still talk about Steven often, as my love for him continues to grow even without him here. *How does love continue to grow, knowing so little about him?* In my favorite picture, Steven was looking at me, and it feels as if we are still communicating with each other the way we did while he was inside of me and in my arms. Frequently, I reread the last few chapters of this book as it makes me feel closer to Steven, but there are always tears that follow. I have not yet accomplished feeling close to Steven without feeling pain.

My mom and I met Aunt Carol last week for lunch, and after a brief catch-up conversation, she asked, "So how is the writing going?"

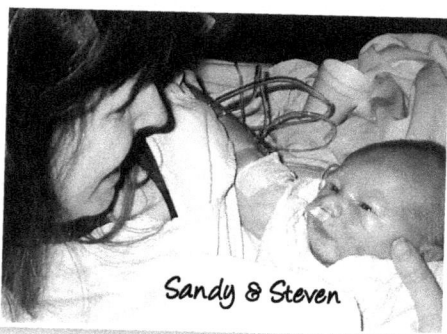

Sandy & Steven

"I haven't been writing much lately." I paused

for a couple of seconds and added, "I don't want the book to be about grief, so I'm only writing once a month."

"What do you want the book to be about?"

It took a moment for me to answer, "I'm still disappointed that it's not about a miraculous healing of Steven's heart. I want to believe this experience has taught me something that I can share with others – one of those important lessons in life – but I haven't figured out what that lesson is, so I can't possibly help others."

"You may not need to figure it all out to help others. Give it some time, and it may become clearer for you."

I sure hope it becomes clearer.

The Great Escape

The kids have been the positive distraction that has helped me through the grief process. Eighteen months old now, they are a lot of fun, but they are also getting into everything. They seem to take turns at being challenging, and this month, Nicolas has me on my toes. Last week, I heard unusual chatter on the baby monitor and decided to take a peek in their room to see what they were up to.

Alexa had her foot stretched up to the top of the side rail, ready to escape. Nicolas had climbed out of his crib and was standing in front of Alexa's crib with his arms cradled to catch Alexa if she tumbled over the rail. There was no way Alexa could lift herself over the rail, but I found it very disturbing that Nicolas had already figured out how to crawl out of his crib and was encouraging his sister to do likewise.

The drama continued when they made their great escape out of the baby-proofed "gated community" in my family room. Once again, Nicolas was the instigator and somehow communicated the plan to Alexa because she was definitely a willing participant. It is hard to explain, but even though their words are not understandable to me, their chatter is more intense when they are talking about something that matters to them. Fortunately for me, I learned to recognize this chatter as something that should matter to me too. *Here we go again!*

As I poked my head around the corner, I watched the whole escape unfold. Nicolas got on his hands and knees near the gate so Alexa could step up on his back and put her foot over the panel of the gate. While she was straddled over the gate, fearful of dropping over and falling, Nicolas moved a toy close to one of the gate panels and in just a couple of seconds, he had stepped on the toy for leverage and hoisted himself over the gate, landing on his feet. He then went to Alexa's aid and carefully pulled her over so she didn't get hurt. As I stared in disbelief, the two of them headed for the kitchen pans for a little noisy playtime.

Positive Insights

In my quest for understanding what we have been through, I feel as though I have found the answer to one big question: *Why did I have to take this journey believing Steven would be healed?* In the past,

I had questioned God for letting so many of us believe a miracle was to come. I wished I could have taken the journey knowing the truth of God's plan for Steven.

I finally came to terms with this after talking with Terri, Grace, and Aunt Carol who had similar responses to this question. *What would this journey have been like with no hope?* To know Steven was destined to die, with no hope of him living, would have made those four months horribly bleak. It would have been a very different journey from the one we took.

Why did I have to take this journey believing that Steven would be healed?

During those four months, I never believed completely that Steven would live, but I did not believe with certainty that he would die either. *I had hope.* A very difficult pregnancy was more bearable because I had hope. And I shared this hope with Steven, and everyone around me.

The other realization was that without the hope that Steven would live, I would not have opted for the C-section during his birth. According to the doctor, my uterus would have burst, causing me serious injury or even death. So I know that I've benefited, people around me have benefited, and ultimately Steven benefited. God knew, and now I know, that hope was critical to this journey. I am ready to finally let go of this question that I have struggled with since the day Steven died. I no longer regret having shared my hopes of a miracle with so many people.

In a recent conversation with a business associate, she commented that it was too bad I didn't know earlier in the pregnancy that we would not be able to donate Steven's organs. Her remark annoyed me because in all that happened, I don't regret my decision to deliver Steven. *He is such an important part of me, and I will forever be changed because of him.*

The conversation made me realize just how much my thinking has changed over time. Back in August, even I questioned why God was asking me to carry a child destined to die. And now I know, without a doubt, that terminating the pregnancy would have been the biggest mistake of my life. *Steven has made me a better person while impacting the lives of so many people who have heard our story.*

God had a plan for Steven from the time of conception.

I also don't have to live with the regret of having aborted the pregnancy and wondering what might have happened if he had been born.

On another positive note, I realize how blessed I am for knowing that God had a plan for Steven from the time of conception. After reading books about other people's grief, I learned that many people struggle with the death of their children, thinking God is in some way punishing them for their sins. Others wonder if their faith is being tested, or even if the devil is responsible.

Fortunate to have never struggled with any of this, I knew from the beginning that God created this child and had a wonderful and glorious promise involving Steven. He also communicated that the path would be very difficult and would take courage and strength. As difficult as it has been for me to comprehend without seeing the whole picture, God's glorious plan involved the death of my son.

He chose Steven to be with Him.

It had nothing to do with punishment, and everything to do with eternal life and a purpose bigger than any of us can imagine. God wanted this journey to unfold just as it did, and I have the peace of knowing Steven is part of His greater plan. I may not understand this great plan, or even agree that it is a great plan. But as I have said many times before, I will have faith in His words until the veil is lifted.

Closer to Knowing It
March 15 – 3 Months

Another month, another milestone. I recently read a book on grief called *Empty Arms* by Pam Vredevelt, written to provide emotional support for those who have suffered a miscarriage, stillbirth, or tubal pregnancy. Not thinking Steven's situation fell into one of those categories, I started the book feeling doubtful about how much it would help. I was even feeling sorry for myself, thinking that thirty-two hours of Steven had to be more difficult than a tubal pregnancy or miscarriages.

As I read through each chapter, there were some very emotional moments as I connected with the author's thoughts on the grieving process. Tears fell, as they often do when I find myself missing Steven so much. But as I read the last two chapters of the book, I came away feeling oddly blessed with my situation. A friend of the author who had miscarried said she would never question the goodness of God for giving her a baby she would never hold. Her baby's life was not long enough to have pictures to carry in her billfold, but it was long enough to fill her heart with wonderful memories.

I felt very different about my situation after reading this from a woman who may never have known whether her child was a girl or a boy. It made me realize how blessed I am for having held Steven for the thirty-two hours that I did. *How fortunate am I that my baby's life was long enough to have pictures with all of my family and to have them hanging in every room in my house! He has a name. He has a face. He is my son. My precious Steven.*

> Some people only dream of angels, but we held one for a day.

For the first time since Steven's death, I am looking at those thirty-two hours as the blessing they actually were. Rather than holding my son for *only* thirty-two hours, I changed my thinking: I was blessed with my son for an *amazing* thirty-two hours. My entire family even got to see and hold Steven during this time. *Some people only dream of angels, but we held one for a day. Thank you, Lord, for those thirty-two hours.*

I will always miss Steven, but my goal is to have good, positive feelings while I miss him. Steven doesn't have to be synonymous with pain and tears. As I wrote earlier, I want to have a smile instead of tears at the mention of Steven's name. Joy instead of pain. Last month, none of this seemed possible. Three months after his birth, I feel hope. I feel hope that I will not always be convincing myself that Steven is a blessing in my life.

I am getting closer to knowing it.

Part of the Master Plan?
April 15 – 4 Months

Four months have passed since I held my son. One hundred twenty days. *Wow. Time has a way of marching on, and I am feeling more comfortable with my new normal.* Getting involved with my business helped me to refocus and get motivated. My babies are doing great and don't allow me to feel sadness for any length of time. They are so happy and full of life. We have been into singing the alphabet lately. I do most of the singing, and they cheer and clap their hands when we are finished.

The other day, I heard a lot of cheering and clapping coming from Nicolas and Alexa's bedroom. When I listened at their door, I heard Alexa saying the handful of letters she knows and then the two of them would start "yeahing" and clapping their hands. Nicolas was squealing with delight. There would be a few second's pause, five or six more letters from Alexa, and more cheering from both of them. It was my first real chuckle since Steven died. *I sure love my kids – all three of them.*

Even though I have started to laugh again, I haven't danced yet, but it is no longer an impossible thought. Steven is still very much a part of my life, but God and time seem to be healing the sad feelings that once overwhelmed me. Now when people ask, I'm able to tell them I have three children without having a complete meltdown. Last week, I heard my mother tell someone she has nine grandchildren. *Steven was number nine.* I just smiled.

I spoke with my sister Cathy on the role of faith in our everyday lives the other day.

"Can you imagine living without having faith that there is a God?" she asked while we were discussing how much our faith has changed over recent years. "Even during our darkest days, our God has a plan, and there is always hope."

I agreed and smiled, thinking back on all of those dark days my God has gotten me through. "Hope is one of God's greatest gifts. It enables us to look beyond circumstances that otherwise seem hopeless."

How would we get through life's challenges with no God, no hope? How could I have endured the last four months of the pregnancy without faith that God had a plan? How could I endure the death of my son without believing he went to a better place?

I was talking to myself as much as to my sister when I said, "Knowing Steven was conceived with a purpose in mind, and having faith that he has been called by One who loves him as dearly as I do – even more than I do – brings a peace to my soul like nothing else can."

Hope.

I've continued to find ways to remember the beautiful baby I miss so much. I sing "Amazing Grace" every morning in the shower. My thoughts are always with Steven when I hear this song, so I decided to sing it to him as a positive way of remembering him. Since I began focusing on only good thoughts involving Steven, I don't feel as much pain when I hear his name or look at his picture. In fact, seeing his picture or thinking of him makes me smile.

There are still times when I cry for him, but I'm okay with this. I don't look at it as a setback in the grieving process anymore. *I'm just missing my son. The loss will always bring tears.* There are happy moments with Steven, and there are also sad ones. Steven is a missing part of me, so I'm sure there will always be happy and sad times.

I've been thinking of a way for Steven's life to impact more people in this world. If I publish this manuscript, I'll donate profits from the book to a children's charity. Steven may not have been able to help children through organ donation, but his story of hope and faith might help even more babies.

Could this be Steven's promise?

In Our Hearts Forever
May 15

We went to the cemetery on Mother's Day. The funeral home had just placed the grave marker. It says "God's Promise" above Steven's name, and "In our arms for a day; In our hearts forever" below his name. There is also an emblem of a child praying. It has been five months since Steven died, but I delayed having the marker placed because I wasn't ready for its finality.

When Tony and I saw it for the first time, he cried. He has not shown much emotion the past few months, and although I know he is grieving, I haven't seen him cry since Steven's funeral. I was surprised that I did not cry when I saw the grave marker.

Oddly enough, these past few weeks, I have been feeling like a part of Steven is just beginning. I even felt compelled to put "God's Promise" on the grave marker, not completely understanding what God's promise for Steven is. *With every day that passes, my belief becomes stronger that the promise will be revealed to us in this lifetime.*

It has been warm the past few days, so the kids and I have been playing outside in the afternoons. "Is that beautiful flower for me?" I asked Alexa as she handed me a flower she had picked from the garden. She eagerly nodded her head, smiling that deliberate smile that she gives me when she has done something good, knowing that hugs and kisses will follow. I grabbed her into my arms, hugging and kissing her, and pulled her onto me as I rolled over backwards. We were both laughing, but she was quick to jump to her feet and check the fate of her flower that I was still holding in my hand.

"No worries, Baby Girl. Our flower is okay. Should we put it in some water?" She nodded as if she knew what I was talking about, and I stood up and walked over to the hose to fill my ice tea cup with water. I handed the flower back to Alexa and she gently put it in the cup of water.

Noticing the attention Alexa was getting, Nicolas headed in the direction of the flowers. A couple minutes later, he walked over to me with his hands clenched tight. When I held out my hand, he opened his fingers to reveal petals from a flower that didn't cooperate. I gave him a big kiss and walked over to the flower cup to put the crushed petals next to Alexa's flower.

Those were a few great moments in an otherwise average day, and I'm learning to appreciate the smaller things in life. Watching my children grow is priceless to me.

I will miss not having these moments with Steven.

Where is the Hope
emerging in your life?

Nicolas

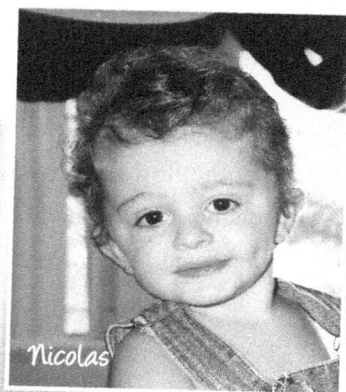

Alexa

Chapter 15

Steven's Hope

"Teach me to do Your will,
for You are my God;
Your Spirit is good.
Lead me in the land
of uprightness."

~ Psalm 143:10 NKJV ~

Steven's Hope for Children
August 15

It was exactly one year ago that we got Steven's fatal diagnosis, and it has been eight months since his death. I sensed that God had big plans for us, but I just never expected changes of this magnitude. So much has happened since May.

In June, I was still researching the idea of publishing this manuscript and donating the profits to a local charity, but I found that selecting a charity was almost as difficult as getting published. After two hours of researching on the computer, I knew my life was about to take a big turn. *I have to talk to Tony about this.*

Tony came home about 6:30 p.m., and when I met him at the door, he sensed immediately that I was up to something.

"So what's up?" He looked around suspiciously.

"I think you should sit down for this one," I was almost breathless with excitement.

Tony let out a sigh as he walked to the couch and sat down. He waited in silence for me to start talking, looking nervous. *He knows this is going to be a life-changer.*

"What do you think about us starting our own non-profit children's charity?"

I couldn't read his expression, and he didn't say anything for several seconds. Uncomfortable with the silence, I quickly added, "We can call it 'Steven's Hope' for all the hope Steven gave us throughout the pregnancy and for the hope it will bring to families with sick children."

"That's not a bad idea," he finally said. I jumped onto his lap and hugged him. *This is it. This is the Hope that was promised.*

We spent the rest of the evening talking about the charity.

Both excited at the idea of charity work, we discussed how our lives would be impacted. Since the twins' birth and Steven's death, our priorities have changed tenfold. Charity work appeals to us now. We feel compelled to make a difference.

It feels like doors are opening, and it is time to take this next big leap of faith. We put a focus group together to gather information and discuss ideas for the charity. Everyone is excited, and the preliminary findings for what programs are needed and where we will implement them seem to be coming together. *Steven's thirty-two hours just might make a difference after all!*

We have decided to focus on families with children who have a critical illness that requires them to remain near the hospital for extended outpatient treatments. We will help families who have children with cancer, who have had transplants, or who are suffering from a serious illness or injury. Our services will include such things as furnished apartments, airfare, meals, transportation, clothing, utilities, and other related expenses. *It is so sad to see how financially and emotionally devastated these poor families are. We can help to off-set that with some resources.*

I pray that with God and Tony beside me, we will somehow figure it out. Tony doesn't seem concerned at all that we will make it a success.

"What if Steven's Hope fails?" I asked after a long day of planning. I had been so excited at the idea of starting the charity that I hadn't stopped to think that it may not be a success. I was overly tired and fear had crept in. The more I researched, the more I realized the need for our services, and I started wondering if we could really make a difference. *I feel like a grain of sand on the beach.*

> *What if Steven's Hope fails?"*

"I don't think it will fail," Tony said with confidence. "We have prayed about this and feel as if God is opening doors, right?" When I didn't answer, he continued, "Think about all of the people who want to get involved, and we haven't even gotten the non-profit paperwork filed yet."

I nodded my head in agreement.

"If God is behind us on this venture, we will succeed," he said as he walked over and gave me a hug. "In fact, I think we will make millions for Steven's Hope for Children!"

I smiled, loving the confidence he has in us. *I wouldn't want to be entering this chapter of my life without him.* After a few seconds of silent embrace, he added, "And besides, if we help one child and one family, we will have done more than most."

"You're right," I quietly answered, still in his arms. "And, oh, how I love the name – Steven's Hope. We will get to hear Steven's name all of the time!" I walked away from him and looked back over my shoulder, "As the charity grows, more and more people will say our son's name. They won't all associate Steven's Hope for Children with the child that once lived, but we will have the satisfaction of knowing the 'Steven' of Steven's Hope for Children is *our* Steven Joseph Cappelli."

"Yes, we will," he softly replied, smiling at me. "Yes, we will."

As I lay in bed that night, I thought about God's incredible ways of working through people. Although He is using Tony and me to get Steven's Hope for Children off the ground, I realized how little control we have over its destiny and the people who will be involved with its success. *We may influence the direction, but I believe it will be much larger than any of us can comprehend at this moment.*

Publishing
August 30

After submitting a brief summary of the manuscript, I received a list with a few agents interested in a book proposal. I also received information suggesting I attend an actual conference next month in Hawaii where I could possibly meet the agents and learn more about writing and publishing books.

> *I will miss them when I go…*

It sounded like fun and would be a great learning experience, but there is so much going on in our lives that I don't feel it's a good time to leave for five days. We are in the middle of tenant improvements on our new insurance agency location, and getting the charity paperwork filed is a priority that has consumed me lately. Not to mention, Nicolas and Alexa just turned two and are a handful for anyone to take care of.

Tony was disappointed when I told him I wasn't going to attend the conference and proceeded to convince me to go with Grace. He will stay and take care of Nicolas and Alexa. I'm excited to be going, but already a little nervous about leaving the kids. They are at an exhausting age, but also a lot of fun. *I will miss them when I go…*

Alexa has new words every day. Lately, she walks around pointing her finger at people and telling them, "I be right back." She walks away for a minute and comes back in the room feeling very important.

And yesterday, I got a painful lesson on what happens when a two-year-old learns how to twist off caps. While putting my makeup on, I looked over to see both of them huddled in a corner of the room. *That is never a good thing.*

"Alexa, what are you up to?" I couldn't see what they were doing from my vanity chair. Silence from both of them. A few seconds later, I asked in a stern voice, "Nicolas, what is Alexa doing?" I wasn't expecting an answer from a couple of two-year-olds, but I hoped it would slow them down while I finished applying my mascara. I looked over to see Nicolas glance up at me with a serious look on his face, and then once again he was engrossed in whatever Alexa was doing.

Quickly finishing my makeup, I walked over to see what they were up to. Alexa had opened the nail polish and was polishing her toe nails. . . and her sandals. . . and the carpet. Nicolas remained in "squat" position, observing every detail, as he often does when Alexa is up to no good.

As I was cleaning the nail polish off the carpet, Alexa climbed on my vanity chair, twisted off the cap to my blush, and began applying blush to her cheeks with my makeup brush. "Alexa, put my makeup brush down," I scolded her and gave up on the carpet to save my makeup. As I pulled her off the chair and collected my makeup, I noticed Nicolas pulling out the safety plugs from an electrical outlet.

"Nicolas, stop, right now!" I yelled, dropped the makeup, and ran toward Nicolas on the other side of the room. While I reprimanded Nicolas and replaced the safety plugs, Alexa moved out of my sight behind the sink. "Alexa, get out here where I can see you," I yelled as I heard the sound of something being dumped on the floor. Grabbing Nicolas under one arm, I reached for the nail polish Alexa had been playing with, and headed in her direction.

In the short time that had passed, she had dumped the trash out of the trash can so that she could use it as a stepping stool, and had climbed up to reach the sink countertop. She twisted off the toothpaste cap and began squeezing a week's worth of toothpaste onto my toothbrush. With a kid under each arm, I headed downstairs to their gated community.

The conference in Hawaii may be just the break I need.

Away from the Family
September 9

The trip to Hawaii was the first time Tony took care of the babies without me around. To my delight, they brought him to his knees more than once.

The first night I was at the conference, he sounded like Mr. Mom when I called to see how his day with the children had gone.

"So how are things going without me?" I asked, hoping to hear that I was being missed.

"We're getting along great," he replied confidently. "I picked the kids up from school and fed them dinner. We played for a while and now they're in bed. I'm just doing a little laundry right now." He sounded way too pleased with himself, and it nauseated me a bit.

"Glad to hear everything is going so well for you all," I lied. I could tell he enjoyed the success of his first day, and I sensed he questioned why I occasionally get so stressed out with our sweet little darlings. *He has no clue. It's just the first day.*

Grace was standing next to me as I hung up the phone. "I guess I'm not needed at home," I said sarcastically. "He seems to have complete control over the situation. He has no idea how exhausting the kids are to take care of every day, and I was hoping this experience might enlighten him to my world of caring for two-year-old twins 24/7."

Grace was amused with my irritation. "I'm sure you will be missed before the conference is over."

The second night I called, Tony still sounded cheerful, but not nearly as confident as the night before. "So what's up around there?" I prodded.

"We're doing okay, but the kids are a little cranky today," he answered. "Apparently, school was a bit of a challenge for both of them. Nicolas kept climbing into Ms. Liberty's cabinet and refused to listen to her when she reprimanded him."

"That doesn't surprise me." I didn't try to hide my amusement.

"Yeah, but the story doesn't end there." Tony sounded tired and a lot less amused. "Alexa felt the need to come to Ms. Liberty's aid by taking matters into her own teeth. The little bite marks in Nicolas' arm were still visible when I picked them up."

"Well, tomorrow is a new day!" I said with optimistic sarcasm. I didn't even try to sound sympathetic. I ended the conversation with,

"Give hugs and kisses to my babies. Love you!"

After finishing the call, I turned to Grace. "Well, he sounded tired tonight. I'm thinking I might be needed…just a little."

"Give him another night or two," was all Grace said as we headed off to dinner.

The third night I called home was Saturday and the first full day (since there was no daycare) that Tony had ever spent with the kids *without me*. He didn't sound very good.

"So what happened?" I asked, a little concerned that Tony sounded so frazzled.

"I'm just so tired. The kids decided to have a 2:00 a.m. get-together and didn't want to go back to sleep. Once they did fall back asleep, I was wide awake. I don't think I fell asleep again until 5:30, and by 6:00, they were rested and ready for a full day of fun and games with Daddy."

"Yeah, sleep deprivation is a real bummer," I said, trying to sound sympathetic.

"Making matters worse, I forgot to put the duct tape on Nicolas' diaper, so my exhausting day started with Nicolas abandoning his dirty diaper. Your mom had to come up and watch them so I could get a little rest."

Thoroughly enjoying the conversation, I struggled to keep my laughter in. Functioning on only a few hours of sleep has become the norm for me; it was funny to me that he was so tired that my mom had to come to his rescue. Still chuckling as I hung up the phone, Grace wanted details.

"Well the funniest part of the conversation is that he forgot the duct tape and Nicolas abandoned his dirty diaper," I said, assuming that sentence would make perfect sense to her.

The top ten reasons to keep duct tape in every room when twins turn two are...

With a blank look on her face, she questioned, "And what does the duct tape have to do with dirty diapers?"

Still smiling at the thought of Nicolas and Tony, I answered. "Duct tape has become a 'staple' in our household. The kids, particularly Nicolas, have taught me many reasons to keep a lot of duct tape on hand."

Grace laughed as I gave her the top ten reasons to keep duct tape in every room when twins turn two. It can be used to:

#10: secure furniture to the walls in their bedroom

#9: tack light switches in the "off" position to conserve energy during the energy crisis

#8 attach the vaporizer onto the furniture that is taped to the wall in their bedroom

#7: tape laptop computers securely to any desk

#6:   cover the manual channel and volume controls on the TV set. This does create a problem if the remote gets lost because removing the duct tape is often messy and sticky. There is also risk that the controls will be damaged and channels can no longer be changed directly from the TV set.

#5:   ensure that alarm clocks control buttons remain as we set them, so that we can wake up at the same time every morning

#4:   disable the faucets in the nearby bathtub, so that the water cannot be turned on and off thirty-five times during your eight-minute shower, causing dramatic changes in the water temperature

#3:   anchor toilet seats so that "Beanie Babies" aren't flushed, causing backed up toilets

#2:   add splashes of color to any room, since duct tape now comes in a variety of colors other than drab gray

And the #1 reason to keep plenty of duct tape on hand?

To prevent "brown-outs" by taping the kids into their diapers. Put a 3"- 4" piece of tape across the front of the diaper holding down the tear-away flaps that release when the diaper is removed. If your child has determination such as Nicolas (or slim hips to wiggle out of the diaper), you can also put a piece of tape on the back of his shirt and attach it to his diaper. By putting his shorts on over the diaper, the tape is barely visible to the naked eye – especially since there are a variety of colors of tape to match his shirts!

After hearing about the familiar challenges of sleep deprivation and "brown-outs" resulting from abandoned diapers, Grace and I went out and toasted Tony's difficult day with a drink.

"There is nothing quite like Mai Tais under the beautiful skies of Hawaii and knowing that your family is missing you." Grace smiled at my comment as we clicked our glasses together and took a sip of our drinks, while enjoying the tropical breezes under the star-filled nights with the sound of the ocean lapping at the beach.

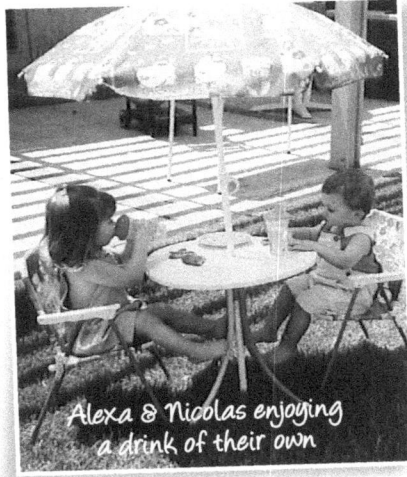

Alexa & Nicolas enjoying a drink of their own

Spinning from all that I learned, I came home from the Maui Writer's Conference excited and hopeful that I am closer to publishing...and missing Tony and my babies. The entire conference was exhilarating. I know getting published is not easy, but I also believe it will happen if God wants it to...*and in His time!*

Have you ever found a way to turn a tragedy into a triumph for others?

Chapter 16

Blessings in the Dark

*"But he said to me,
'My grace is sufficient for you,
for my power is made
perfect in weakness.'"*

~ 2 Corinthians 12:9 NIV ~

Please Grant Me Patience
September 25

This has been an overwhelming couple of weeks, but not because of what is happening in my life. It is because of what is happening across the country and around the world. Two weeks ago, there was a terrorist attack in the United States that took the lives of many Americans. It is hard to express the sadness and fear so many of us feel. *It all seems so senseless – such a waste of life.*

Details of the attack are being replayed over and over on the TV. The morning it happened, I watched from my television set and felt sheer terror as the details unfolded before my eyes. *I can only imagine the horror of those who experienced it firsthand.* So many people are asking "Why?" I'm sure many who have suffered personal loss are questioning God with hurt and anger similar to what I felt after Steven's death.

Since the attack, I've found myself consumed again with death and eternity. Nothing else seems important at times like these. *The thought of eternity makes situations like this much more bearable.*

Kim received another word for me within days of this horrific event. We haven't talked much this past year, so I was surprised to hear from her. She hasn't sent me any words since the one a few days after Steven's funeral telling me a promise is still to come.

"Hey, Kim. It's good to hear your voice!"

"Yeah, it has been a long time. You guys are always in my thoughts." She sounded a little depressed.

"Is everything okay with all of you?"

"It has been a really tough year for us, but we're all okay."

We talked for a while, and I realized the toll Steven's death has taken on her faith. She sounded like she is moving forward just as I am, but it saddened me to hear the challenges she is facing. The terrorist attack was just more bad news, and I pray that God gives her the strength to get through each day.

Right before we ended our call, she said, "I received another word for you. I just emailed it to you."

I didn't ask for details on the phone, but immediately went to check my email after we hung up. We never talked about the terrorist attack or all the thoughts on eternity that I've been consumed with, so the relevance of the words I read in the email surprised me. Some of what she heard and had emailed me seemed to be answering my questions:

> "…I am the Light; I am Life. In Me, there is eternity, yet the world only sees the now. The promise is eternity in a kingdom of the everlasting one true God. The enemy thinks through death he has won, yet in Me there is no death, only eternal life away from suffering and pain…"

Eternity is something I have always believed in, but never spent much time thinking about. Believing in eternity has always been better than the alternative, so I never questioned it. In my mind, they were words to comfort people who grieve the loss of a loved one. After the death of my son and the many lives lost in the terrorist attack, words that speak of eternity are taking on new meaning.

I wonder if Kim's word has something to do with the confusion I have been feeling lately with all of the turmoil around us. Even though eternal life is the wonderful promise God offers us, I still feel confusion as to what eternity has to do with the journey I have been on with Steven.

I want so badly to believe that Steven's Hope for Children is God's promise for my son, and yet, I feel I may be off track. I have an unsettling feeling that God is trying to communicate to me that there is more to His promise for Steven, but I don't understand.

It is disappointing to feel confidence in what God might be communicating one day, only to be filled with doubt the next. Faith is frustrating. During the past couple of days, I have been trying to put a book proposal together for publishers, but have been too confused to do it. I was excited when I saw a happy ending on the horizon with Steven's Hope for Children, but now, I don't know. I'm so desperate for clarity and direction.

> *Dear God,*
>
> *I am feeling a little sad today because I feel I'm no closer to understanding Your promise for Steven. I know Your plan will bring joy, and I should not feel sad. I'm sorry for my impatience and ignorance. I am so desperate for an understanding that I can comprehend. Steven's Hope for Children is something that makes sense to me; I hoped it was an answer coming from You.*

But deep within, I sense it is my reason more than Yours. Or maybe it is only part of the promise. Either way, I don't feel the peace I need to move forward.

I don't want to make the same mistake again. I originally thought a miraculous healing of Steven's heart was Your promise; now I want to believe it is Steven's Hope for Children. I know I can't handle more grief, so I will try to sit back and be patient.

At times, I find myself believing the promise is something specific to my journey with Steven. Other times, it seems to be much bigger, as if it is a promise for all of mankind. Is the promise a life with You in eternity? I'm only beginning to comprehend how huge Your gift of eternity is for all of us.

I think eternity is a wonderful promise for all of mankind, but what does it have to do with this journey that I have been on with Steven? I know Steven is with You in heaven, so a promise involving Steven and eternity confuses me. My thinking and ways are so simple compared to yours. I pray that You open doors soon that will bring clarity to my journey.

I talked to Grace shortly after writing this letter to God and she commented, "Stay focused with Steven's Hope for Children because I believe it is part of God's plan, even if it is not the 'promise' you had in mind for Steven."

"Yeah," I reluctantly agreed. "I just feel such confusion right now. I hate the uneasy feelings I have and wish I had confidence in the direction I should take."

"We don't always know what God's plan is, but give it time. I think it will become clearer for you. Just keep walking through doors that open." Then, with a little sarcasm, she added, "You know, patience has never been one of your virtues."

I smiled. *She's right. I always want the answer yesterday.*

On A Lighter Note
November 20

The kids are two years old and have been in preschool part time for three months now. They seem to really like it. Nicolas' curly brown hair and dimples get him a lot of attention from his teacher, which he loves. I usually pick them up during reading time, and both of my kids are always sitting on the teacher's lap while the other children sit on the floor in front of her. She told me that every time she sits down with a book, my kids come running up to her to sit on her lap. I laughed because having both of them on my lap is their routine at home when we read books.

Alexa already sings the alphabet and knows her numbers through fifteen. They are not always in the correct order, but she is getting closer. She is also learning new songs every week at school and loves to sing them all of the time. It is not uncommon for me to wake up at 3:00 in the morning to her little voice singing, "a moo

moo here and a moo moo there. . ."

I also love the honesty that comes with all her new words and sentences. Communicating with words is so new to both of them, they would never think to lie. A few days ago, they were playing in their bedroom and I heard Nicolas start to cry. When I walked in the room, a tearful Nicolas was waving his injured finger at me.

"What happened?" I asked as I kissed his finger.

Alexa was standing next to him and informed me, "He got bit."

A little surprised, I turned to Alexa. "How did he get bit?" There was silence, as if she did not completely understand what I said. More directly, I asked, "Did you bite Nicolas?"

She nodded and happily answered "Yes!" She seemed pleased that she understood my question and happy to have enlightened me on the situation.

Nicolas is still not talking much, but seems to be enjoying pre-school just as much as Alexa. We receive daily report sheets from the teacher telling us how each child's day was, how they felt, and what they ate. Alexa's always says "happy and playful." After the first couple of weeks, we noticed most of Nicolas' daily reports had changed from "happy and playful" to "happy and outgoing."

Being a proud papa, Tony was going around telling everyone that Nicolas is "outgoing" at school. I happened to notice that on all of his "outgoing" reports, there was usually a comment on the bottom of the paper with statements such as, "likes to climb on table and jump off," or "likes to play in mud," or "likes to put spaghetti on his head."

I told Tony we needed to get a clearer definition of "outgoing." What we both interpreted from the teacher's vague explanation is that "outgoing" and "disturbing the class" go hand in hand.

Nicolas, Sandy & Alexa

Yesterday, I got a report on him that said he was "excited" instead of outgoing. I didn't ask.

It's Been a Year
December 27

This month has been challenging, but with the help of family and friends, I am surviving. I've been battling depression with the one-year anniversary of Steven's birth and death. The week before Steven's birthday, I decided to see a grief counselor for the first time since Steven died. I was hoping she could help me channel some of the sad, anxious feelings I have been having lately.

"I thought that by now, I would be past some of these feelings," I said, after giving the counselor a brief summary of my journey. "It seemed like I had made so much progress over the past months, and now all of this depression and anxiety... I don't know what to think."

She just listened, so I continued. "It seems like I take three steps forward and then two steps back. Most of the time, I feel focused and excited about what my future holds. Other times, like today, I feel frayed, insecure, and tired."

"It is very normal to have these feelings near the anniversary of a person's birth and death. It is a process that takes a lot of time. Try not to put a time frame on your grief."

We talked a little about God, which eventually led us to the topic of Steven's Hope and all of my anxiety over such a big endeavor. It is officially a corporation, and now we are filing for tax-exempt status. As we get closer to opening our doors, I am feeling nervous about where this new path will lead us.

> I've been battling depression with the one-year anniversary of Steven's birth and death.

"I believe God is leading you somewhere, and you should continue to walk through doors that open," she said after hearing about the charity. She was nice-looking woman with long brown hair that rested on her shoulders. Her office was cheerful and bright, and I found it easy to relax around her.

Although depression brought me in, I found myself enjoying the conversation that revolved around Steven. *I don't have a reason to talk about him, and it feels good to tell someone who doesn't know our story.*

"I just wish God would make things clearer to me. Nothing, including answers for what the purpose of this journey has been about, is happening fast enough. Clarity after all this time is still missing." *I sound defeated, don't I?*

"Maybe you should 'go with the flow' a little more, and think a little less about the details. So much of your frustration seems to come when you want answers to difficult questions. See where this path leads you, and answers may follow. Time will bring a healing and answers to many of your questions. Steven is putting you on a different path, but God will bring you peace..."

Not up for a lecture on God, I interrupted her. "I know that what you are saying makes sense," I knew I sounded impatient, "but when I look back on all that has happened over the past three years, I see good things and believe my life will be on a very different course because of it all. In fact, I think Steven's greatest gift to me is making me 'forever different.' I have new goals, ambitions, and priorities. God has a much more significant place in my life and in my heart. And I'm looking to new levels for fulfillment and meaning in life."

Pausing for just a moment, I quietly added, "But the healing process is so painfully slow."

We talked for a few minutes about the manuscript and whether I might pursue publication.

"I think you should at least finish the manuscript. You can decide whether to publish at a later time."

"But Steven's story would be easier told in the past tense after I am certain of the outcome and clearly understand the promise."

She was quick to reply. "It may be less stressful to tell your story in hindsight. But knowing the answers requires no faith."

"I know faith brings strength, but lately, I seem to have misplaced faith with fear," I admitted.

I know faith brings strength but lately, I seem to have misplaced faith with fear.

After leaving her office, I continued to reflect on what she said. She recognized my issues with control and patience right away, and stressed that I should work on my control issues and continue to take one day at a time. *Nothing she said was all that enlightening, but I'll probably see her a few more times.* Even when her comments are things I already know, they take on new meaning coming from a professional.

The other benefit to talking with her is that I'm able to talk about my child who still feels so important to me, but is seldom thought about by anyone else. *Hopefully, these insecure feelings will pass with the start of a new year.*

My session with the counselor helped put things back into perspective. *We can't always be focused and in control.* Lapses like I have had these past few weeks are normal and shouldn't deter me from my ultimate goals. They are just a part of life. Focusing more on the lesson I can learn rather than the setback itself is something I will try to do. If I can redirect my fears to God instead of trying to carry the load alone, these insecure feelings will subside.

A week after my session with the grief counselor, I was facing Steven's birthday. The counseling helped me get through the week because I better understood that the sadness I was experiencing was just a normal part of the grieving process. Friends and family also helped me survive the dark days by sending cards and emails, letting me know their thoughts were with us. *It is good to know people haven't forgotten Steven.*

My entire family went to the cemetery on Steven's birthday and we placed a small Christmas tree on his grave. We sang Christmas carols and remembered our beautiful boy. It was a special day. Nicolas and Alexa had so much fun playing and singing that the mood was not somber. Their laughter lightened everyone's mood.

Steven is buried in a section of the cemetery for babies and small children, so a lot of the graves had Christmas decorations and small toys on them. Two of my nieces chased after Nicolas and Alexa as they tried to take the decorations off the other children's graves.

It was a beautiful sunny day, and the presence of God was everywhere. Although I'm doubtful I ever will be happy about decorating my child's grave, there is a knowing in my heart that Steven is where he needs to be.

Christmas was good in a bittersweet way. Although the ache for Steven never left, I found myself consumed with the wonderment of two-year olds and Christmas. The lights, snowmen, and Christmas trees (or "nomen" and "mistris trees" as Alexa calls them), Santa Claus, and Baby Jesus in the manger. Everything is so new and exciting to them.

Thank you, Lord, for this family that brings me such joy. I am so blessed.

What are some of the blessings in your life?

Chapter 17

The Revelation

"For God so loved the world that He gave His only begotten Son, that whoever believes in Him should not perish but have everlasting life."

~ John 3:16 NKJV ~

God's Promise for Steven
January 15

It is the middle of January, and I am excited about all of the possibilities the New Year holds. The depression from last month seems to have faded, and everything is looking brighter.

I continue to move forward with Steven's Hope for Children and in my quest to find answers and meaning to all that has happened...and all that awaits us. I am feeling a new peace after an incredible revelation that came while reading another book on eternity. In part, I read about eternity in search of answers for Steven's life, but mainly I read about heaven because it is full of promise. *I can't seem to learn enough about it.*

Recently, while skimming a book on infant death, I was unprepared for my emotional reaction. I went numb after reading a chapter in a book titled *"One Minute After You Die"* by Erwin W. Lutzer. It took me a few days to comprehend the magnitude of what those few words mean to me.

The author was explaining how the death of an infant opens the hearts of their loved ones to the realization that we are all headed toward home. As I read the words he quoted by James Vernon McGee, I felt a tingling sensation throughout my body. It was as if the words were speaking to me with incredible clarity:

> **"When a shepherd seeks to lead his sheep to better grass up the winding, thorny mountain paths, he often finds that the sheep will not follow him. They fear the unknown**

ridges and the sharp rocks. The shepherd will then reach into the flock and take a little lamb on one arm and another on his other arm. Then he starts up the precipitous pathway. Soon the two mother sheep begin to follow, and afterward the entire flock. Thus they ascend the tortuous path to greener pastures.

So it is with the Good Shepherd. Sometimes He reaches into the flock and takes a lamb to Himself. He uses the experience to lead His people, to lift them to new heights of commitment as they follow the little lamb all the way home."

A little later in the chapter, he continued saying that a child's short life can fulfill the will of God. Although we don't understand it, that little one has finished the work God has given him to do. Though now in heaven, the child continues his or her ministry through the lives of parents and relatives.

After reading these words, I sat for several minutes unable to move. My whole body was tingling, and I had to focus on breathing. It was a huge revelation. It should have been obvious after all this time, but until I saw the words before me, I had not been able to comprehend it.

> *What if the journey is the very reason for his life?*

What if this journey of faith and all that transpires because of it is not merely the <u>result</u> of Steven's death as we have assumed? What if the journey is the very reason for his life?

Closure
January 20

I can honestly say that reading those words has brought some peace and understanding. They would not have made sense or brought me comfort immediately after Steven's death, but they do bring peace after searching for a purpose and becoming so much closer to God throughout the entire process.

I feel as though I have followed God in search of answers for Steven's brief life all the way to heaven's door!

With this new understanding of God and where we are headed after life on earth, I know there is a purpose for Steven's life. His thirty-two hours on earth fulfilled the will of God and so he went home to live with Him for eternity. His ministry has been left to Tony, me, Steven's Hope for Children, and all who believe in what Steven's life represents.

I will continue to seek answers from God, but I no longer feel that I am on a quest to understand His promise for my son. I believe the charity is only one part of the promise; in fact, the promise could be something different to each person that is impacted in some way by Steven's life.

Does this revelation mean I will miss Steven any less? No, I will miss him every minute of every day I am without him. But, I can finally answer two of the questions I couldn't before:

1.   Do I know without a doubt the true blessing Steven is to my family and me? *YES! I now know how blessed I am to have held Steven for just a day in this lifetime.*

2.   Could there be promise in the death of a child? *Without a doubt, I know there is promise for every child of God, even in death. Whether it is Steven's legacy on earth, or knowing how blessed I will be when I hold him for all of eternity, I will never doubt God's promise for my son.*

Steven continues to touch so many. A couple of weeks ago, a stranger to me but a friend of Aunt Carol's spoke to me at my cousin's wedding. She had read a portion of this manuscript, and said that her faith has been changed forever. Her comments on my book surprised me, and although I wanted details, I just thanked her.

Thinking about what she had said, I had trouble comprehending that someone I didn't know could be interested in my story. It was such an odd feeling to have impacted a complete stranger, and it was then that I realized we may never know how many people Steven's life touches.

At this point, God has given us some answers, but has mostly given us faith. I don't think He wants us to have all of the answers to His promise for Steven because we would no longer need faith. His ultimate promise to all of us is eternity, and I believe His promise for Steven involves reaching more of His children through this child who lived for just one day.

> God reached
> Tony and me
> through
> Steven in a
> way that
> traditional
> religious
> teachings
> could not.

God reached Tony and me through Steven in a way that traditional religious teachings could not. Our family and friends have followed us on this journey and have also experienced a more personal God. Many more will be taken on the same road we have traveled through this book. I'm not sure who will be impacted by Steven's story, but I am certain that what is powered by God will reach those who can benefit from it.

The irony to the conclusions I have made involving God's promise for Steven is that they revolve around the same promise of eternal life that He has made to everyone who believes in Him and asks for His grace. Salvation is for anyone who recognizes their sin and acknowledges their need for salvation. *All we have to do is ask.*

It seems so easy, and yet when we give our hearts to the Lord, we are forever changed. The way we view eternal life determines the way we view death and ultimately the way we live our lives. Conversations, goals, and motives shift with the awareness of His everlasting reward. We spread the good news of Christ because we long to fill heaven with our family and friends.

And to think a little over a year ago, I questioned why God was asking me to carry a child that would die only hours after birth. I, like the rest of the world, "only saw the now." I never thought about heaven and eternity until the circumstances of this past year forced me to.

After Steven's death, I didn't regret having given him life because I had been changed so much by the experience. But I finally realized that even though I only had him for one day in this life, I will have him for all of eternity in the next life. It has finally sunk in. *Our lives are so short and insignificant compared to what lies ahead. When the end finally comes, so much is just beginning.*

Something I once said with a heavy heart to cope with my grief is now my inspiration for living a very different life. I am smiling as I write these words for the last time: *It is only goodbye for now, my sweet child!*

Alexa decorating Steven's grave.

Steven

As I look toward heaven and whisper your name

So many things I'd like to say:

Are you growing? Are you happy?

Can you feel my love each day?

Do you hear the songs I sing you

When I'm by myself,

Gazing at your picture

On the bedroom shelf?

Your brother and sister miss you too

They send you their balloons;

With pictures and notes scribbled inside

Hoping you'll come back soon.

Every night I pray to Him

"Take care of my little one."

"And, Jesus, give him hugs from Mommy."

Do you get them, my sweet son?

No home runs; No touchdown passes

No roars from the crowd;

But knowing your life has touched so many

Makes your daddy proud.

I've come so far these past few years

Dealing with my sorrow;

The hope you bring to all of us

Keeps me moving toward tomorrow.

You're a gift from God, my little angel

You fill my heart with joy.

You have changed my life, my thoughts, my dreams

My precious little boy.

I'm a better person for missing you

Though we won't always be apart;

I'll do my best to live without you

While I hold you in my heart.

Goodbye for now, my sweet child,

Mommy

Sandy Cappelli

Have you allowed God to show you the treasures within the tragedy for you?

Conclusion

The Ripples 10 Years Later

"God is looking for ordinary people empowered by Him to do extraordinary things!"

~ Author Unknown ~

A decade has passed, and I'm finally slowing down long enough to finish the final chapter.

This incredible journey with all of its blessings and challenges continues to unfold. In my wildest dreams, I never imagined the changes we would experience or how this book would end. In the beginning, I had my own ideas of how my life should go and what my book should be about. In fact, one of the reasons it has taken me ten years to publish is because this was *not* the story I wanted to write…or publish.

But today, I am not the same woman who began the journey with so many opinions of how it should end. I have been touched and inspired by God. Brought to my knees so many times, I decided to fight less and trust more. The truth is that when we trust, regardless of the circumstance, He makes all things beautiful in His time.

The power of God's promise of eternal life for Steven and each one of us never leaves my thoughts. Although I still grieve my loss, I no longer grieve with despair.

I am grieving with the hope of God's promise, knowing each day that passes is one day closer to being with my son...and God's Son.

Nick (rarely Nicolas anymore) and Alexa are twelve years old, and continue to bring me incredible joy. They are beautiful children with beautiful spirits, and I never take for granted what a gift they are to all of us. They have been raised with God in their hearts, and it is easy to see Him in everything they do. *I am so proud to be their mother.* Alexa has an amazing voice and spends most of her spare time in musical theatre. She recently won Upland Idol, a vocal competition in our city, which has opened doors for other singing opportunities. Nick still loves to entertain everyone and wants to be an actor or comedian. Both kids lead worship in the kid's ministry at the Christian church we've attended since they were in preschool.

Kim and I have remained close. She has continued to be my prayer warrior, and I still find myself in awe of her faith in God. Kim's latest calling has been to welcome a family with seven orphaned children from Ethiopia into her home to be raised as her own. It has been a year-long process, but they should be arriving in the next few weeks.

We make a point to travel to Colorado every year or two during summer vacations, and Nick and Alexa love to visit Kim and play with her children and grandchildren. As toddlers, Nick and Alexa called her their "Fairy God Mother." From a very young age, they were told their birth involved God, Mommy, Daddy, and Kim, but it has only been in recent months that they are beginning to comprehend the miracle of their birth. As they mature, they will understand the magnitude of Kim's gift of life and what it has meant to our family.

My parents are doing well, and my sweet mother continues to be my biggest support. In fact, I'm not sure Steven's Hope for Children would have survived without her being such a significant person in our lives. She volunteers every day at the charity and also makes all the connections for Nick and Alexa that I'm unable to make with my hectic schedule. Whenever I'm stuck, she is ready to jump in as she has done for me my entire life. The kids adore her.

Grace has also been a huge support to us and the charity. Like my mother, she has been involved in almost all of Nick's and Alexa's activities. She has also been a huge support to Steven's Hope for Children, backing us financially and helping with all of our events. This past year, she has had her life turned upside down with her own personal battle with stage-four cancer. Her faith in God throughout her ordeal has been such an inspiration to everyone around her. In a conversation we recently had, she mentioned how much the journey with Steven changed her own faith, directly impacting and bringing her strength in fighting her own battle.

We will never know the ripples of Steven's life and all of those who have been impacted.

Steven would have turned eleven last December. We continue to celebrate his birthday every year at the cemetery by singing Christmas carols and decorating a tree in his memory. I still sing "Amazing Grace" to him almost every day. The ache in my heart from missing him has never left, but life is so much richer because of him.

The lives of my family are richer because of him. The lives of the Steven's Hope families are richer because of him.

Steven's Hope for Children

The awareness of death is humbling, and yet it is this awareness that challenges us to live more memorable lives. I'm no longer looking for my life to get back to normal – not because it is not possible – but because I now understand that *normal is not good enough*. I want our lives to be extraordinary in God, which is anything but normal in today's world. *I am leaving normal behind.*

Even with our open hearts and minds, the road we have taken since Steven's death has not been an easy one. But with every door that opens, we become more committed to the cause. Seeking answers for Steven's short life is no longer the motivation behind the effort.

Tony and I have found that reprioritizing what is important and devoting ourselves to something that gives us purpose has made life much more meaningful. *What good is it if we are successful in things that don't matter?* But even with determined spirits, it is easy to get derailed with the busyness and challenges of life. Every day, we have to ask God to bring us compassion in the small things... to break our heart for what breaks His. It is so easy for us to forget.

Steven's Hope for Children has come a long way from that first year when we assisted three families. We threw a stone in calm water a long time ago and created ripples. As people got on board to help us, we began to see change. And it is an awesome experience to see what can be accomplished when people pull together for a cause. In fact, last year we helped over 1,600 children through our three programs! The families come from California, across the United States, and internationally.

Steven's Hope for Children has the "Housing for Hope" program where we rent apartments for families needing extended outpatient care after transplants and cancer treatments. We have plans for our own facility, but that has not yet come to fruition.

Once again, God's timing, not mine.

Through our "Fill a Need" program, we feed, clothe, provide transportation, and help with a variety of needs a family struggling with a sick child is faced with.

Our third program "We Care" helps with the emotional support during this challenging time. We provide meals, gifts, parties, entertainment, prayer, and many other areas of support through this program. In fact, our "We Care Winter Wonderland Project" alone provided over $65,000 worth of gifts to six hospitals last year.

In the past two years, we started two children's boutiques of new and gently-used children's items and opened it to the public to help fund the programs. Not only do these stores help needy families in our community with low-cost clothing, a ripple effect of these boutiques is that we were able to expand our "Fill a Need" program with a project called "Klothing Kids." Through the "Klothing Kids Project," we give gift cards to social workers so needy families burdened with a child's illness can shop for clothes for free. We will help hundreds of children this year alone through this project.

Even with the steady growth of Steven's Hope for Children, it has been a challenging decade, both emotionally and financially. *I don't think God wants life to be easy, so I quit looking for easy.* I've learned to lean on Him through the good and bad, and I believe that is exactly what He wants from all of His children – for us to need and depend on Him.

What has changed the most in this past decade is my heart to serve. The more God uses me to help others, the more I want to do. *It is an incredible feeling to be the answer to a prayer.* And that is exactly what Steven's Hope for Children has become to so many people in need.

We are making a difference, one child and one family at a time. And with each family that comes to us, there is a story that comes with them. I never know who will be impacted more – them or us.

One eighteen-year-old girl, Maria, came for treatment for a brain tumor with no parent or relative with her. It was a strange situation for Steven's Hope because we help children through age eighteen, but this was the first time there was a child in our apartment by herself. Her mother was a single mother and had to stay with her four other children, ranging from two to fifteen years of age. They were very poor and had no friends or relatives that could come to California with Maria.

We flew her out from Texas so she could receive the life-saving treatment and realized Steven's Hope would become her temporary home, and we would become her temporary parents to get her through one of the most challenging times of her life. I have to admit, her Texas charm made it easy. *She had no idea how her challenges and positive outlook inspired everyone who met her.* Volunteers from Steven's Hope took turns spending time with her between treatments. She went with us to sporting events, church, parties, and even saw the beach for the first time.

The story would have ended there, but when she finished treatment and went back to Texas, she turned nineteen, lost her insurance, and still needed another surgery. She called one of the volunteers she had become close to, and together we flew her back to California. She was no longer able to receive benefits from Steven's Hope due to her age, but she moved in with Tony, the kids, and me and became a part of our family. Nick and Alexa thought of her as their big sister. She

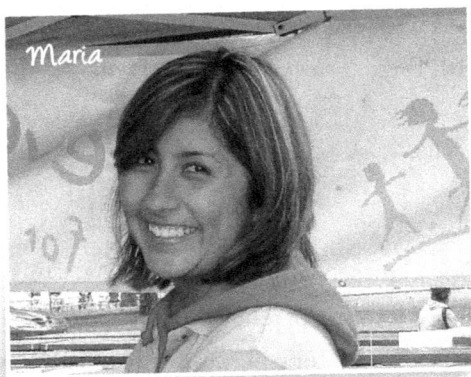

volunteered at Steven's Hope while we got her the medical care she needed over several months.

We had hoped she would stay in California and go to school, but that was my plan and not hers. She lived with us for nine months, went to church with us, camped with us, and experienced things she would never have been able to otherwise. A few months after her surgery, she moved back to Texas. Although it was hard for us to see her go, we knew we had served God's purpose in her life. We were an answer to her prayer, but the reality was that everyone who met Maria benefited from her courageous spirit. She was an inspiration to all of us.

We receive letters of gratitude from so many of the families we help, and it reminds me to appreciate life and the fragility of it. It is so easy to get caught up in the chaos of everything happening at Steven's Hope, always wanting to do more, that I have to remind myself to slow down and be grateful for all that we have accomplished through the power and mercy of God. Below is a letter I received from a woman whose grandson, Xander, was being treated for a brain tumor.

Hi Sandy,

I don't really know where to start......You, your foundation have made such a difference in what we have had to go through......First finding out Xander had a brain tumor.... Christie calling me from Loma Linda that day, in such tears I could hardly understand her....Me trembling to the point of almost passing out.....A few days later Xander having brain surgery.....Being told he may never swallow again, move his limbs...the list goes on.....and then Xander waking up from surgery, kicking and screaming....His neurosurgeon with tears in his eyes, saying he's never seen such an amazing little boy... ...He called Xander a miracle ....

Finally, Xander was going to be discharged, but having to drive so far and him having to have thirty-three radiation treatments before we could go home…we all were so blessed to find out about you…….It felt like we were sinking and you came along and pulled us up, saved us…..we were able to live as a family after months of being in the hospital, separated…..This is the difference Steven's Hope made in this journey….

When Xander got sick, we had quite a few family members and friends surround us….As time went on, most have disappeared, leaving the impact on Christie and myself….Christie and I both have said that we have found more support and caring from total strangers……People who know what we have been through…..Not leaving us, but surrounding us…..There haven't been a lot of people in my life who have made great differences – touched me so much as you have….

God brought us together, Sandy, I have no doubt……Tony was so right when he said to me, "God may not give you what you want, but He gives you what you need." God brought Steven's Hope to us knowing you and your foundation were what we needed…..He puts people in your life for a reason, and at the right times….people who come into your life, who were never there to show you hope, strength, hold your hand, making the difference in surviving your darkest time, God's chosen few… this is you, my friend……I believe in angels, and you will always be an angel to us……what Steven's Hope is all about….. You have touched our hearts…..

Even though this chapter is coming to an end, Xander still has a long way to go……but knowing there is Steven's Hope makes what we face in the future less difficult, knowing you will be there once again to see us through another difficult time, once again holding our hands.

God Bless you, Cheryl

Xander

Cheryl's letter is just a reminder of why we do what we do every day. In the middle of their pain, we have an opportunity to make a difference.

One of the many lessons I have learned over the years is that we may never know the ripple effect of our actions. Sometimes even a small gesture can have an incredible impact on someone's life.

As challenging as this can be in our busy lives, I believe it is critical that we carve out time in our hectic day to be silent so we can hear the whisper of God. And more importantly, when we get those whispers or promptings, we need to take that leap of faith, even when the outcome seems unclear. *Sometimes we need to throw that stone in calm water just to see what happens – if for no other reason than to never look back and wonder things like, "What if I had started that charity after Steven died? I wonder if we could have helped a few children." I know the answer to that question.*

We all have "what if's" in our lives, but since Steven's death, I have fewer. I know life goes by in a blink, it can be taken away in an instant, and sometimes we don't get second chances to make a difference.

It brings me incredible joy that so many lives are being impacted by Steven's short life. The ultimate satisfaction comes from knowing that his life might even strengthen a person's faith or bring someone on the fence a little closer to our One True God.

There was a time I thought Steven's thirty-two hours of life weren't long enough to make a difference. His life was so important to me, but I feared others would forget. Now I know differently. Through Steven's Hope for Children, he will be remembered by many of us for years to come. The best part for me is that, in addition to helping children and their families, I also have a reason to say my son's name every day.

Although I don't have Steven to hold in my arms, his promise lives on in all who are impacted by his life. From the people I have met through Steven's journey and this book, to the courageous families we have helped through Steven's Hope for Children, to all of the wonderful friends, supporters, and volunteers who have come into my life – these are the ripples of Steven's life.

And what a wonderful promise for this child of mine!

Tony, Alexa, Sandy & Nick

What breaks your heart – what is it that God may be asking you to be a part of and make a difference? What if you could see the ripples of your life? ...What would you see?

Would you consider...
Helping us to Ripple It Forward?

Did this book move you emotionally? Do you think this message can help in someone's healing process? If you do, and would like to help create a ripple in the life of people who can benefit from this book, please visit us at www.SandyCappelli.com/RippleItForward. By making a tax-deductible donation to Steven's Hope for Children through this link, you can sponsor one or more books to be given, free of charge, to a person involved in the Steven's Hope ministry who needs to hear this message. This outreach is made possible by generous people who want to make a difference, one life and ripple at a time.

If this story has impacted you in any way, please visit me at www.SandyCappelli.com or email me at Ripples@SandyCappelli.com to share your story.

Thank you for being a part
of our ripple!

About Sandy Cappelli

Inspirational speaker and author Sandy Cappelli is on a mission to create ripples of impact and inspire others to do the same. Having walked a journey of faith through infertility, in vitro fertilization, miraculous conception, and then the birth and death of her son, she is determined to help others walk their own journeys, rediscover God's promises, and begin to transform their challenges and tragedies into powerful ripples that will change the world one life at a time.

Sandy is the co-founder and Vice President of Steven's Hope for Children, a non-profit that supports families with seriously ill children. With a Master's Degree in Business Administration, twenty years of successful ownership of an insurance agency, and multiple awards recognizing her commitment to the community and families in crisis, she has decided to share her message of "God's Promises and Our Ripples."

She currently lives in Southern California with her husband and two children.

Stay tuned for home study courses, workbooks, and programs designed to support others through their journeys of questioning and strengthening their faith.

About Steven's Hope for Children

Through its programs, Steven's Hope is impacting lives of families. But Steven's Hope is more than helping with temporary housing, food, clothing, and other expenses. It is a community of caring, compassion, and support for families facing incredible challenges. It is a haven for families to have options for care and treatment, love, and a belief that anything is possible.

Vision Statement

That no family be left alone during their time of a child's health crisis

Mission Statement

To support the families of seriously ill or injured children during a child's extended treatment and care

Core Values

Faith makes all things possible.
Embrace hope.
Cherish family.
Be responsible for each other.
Treat everyone with respect.
Encourage personal growth.
Do more with less.
Be humble.
Help those in need.
Make ripples.

Between hospital and home,
there is hope.®

Steven's Hope.®

For more information on
Steven's Hope for Children,
or to make a donation,

Visit our website at:
www.StevensHope.org

Or contact us at:
Info@StevensHope.org

Acknowledgments

To my sweet mother and nana to our children, Marilyn Gengler: You are one of God's greatest gifts to me. Thank you for being beside me every step of the way. I love you so much.

To my prayer warrior, Kim Nuss: You introduced me to a God I never knew...and rocked my world. I am forever indebted to you.

To my aunt and special friend, Grace Vick: Through the entire journey, you have been with me. We laughed, cried, and grew in faith together. I will treasure you always.

To my aunt and uncle and spiritual mentors, Jack and Carol Distaso: You both have taught me that "God Is." Through the good and the bad, your faith is unshakeable. You bring God's word to so many.

To my dad and sisters, Pete Gengler, Cathy Carter, Lori Patterson, and Julie Jensen: Thank you for being there when I needed you. I have always been able to count on each of you.

To my very good friend, Terri Ellison: Our friendship has stood the test of time.

To all my family and friends who have traveled this journey with me: Thank you for your love and support through the good and the bad. It has been, and continues to be, an incredible journey.

To my newest BFF, Diana Arnold: You are a very special ripple that emerged from this journey. Thank you for your friendship and your belief in this book. The time spent together was as fun as reaching our destination. Let's do it again!

To my editor, Amanda Johnson, founder of True to Intention: You and your team of coaches and editors gave me the confidence I needed to share my story with the world. Thank you for your insight, nudges, friendship, and patience. You are an inspiration to so many of us.

To a friend who made a difference, Debbie Bajenaru: You lit the fire beneath me when you pulled your friends together to read my manuscript. Your involvement, by taking time out of your busy life to push this project forward, was the basis for me taking the next step in this journey of faith. Thank you.

To Doleen Borba: Thank you for reaching out and making a difference during some of my darkest days.

I would also like to thank the many people, some of whom I have never met, who read my manuscript before it was published and encouraged me to move forward with publishing. The time and energy you put into reading and making comments were extraordinary gifts to me. You were all part of the ripple.